FRIENDSHIP MARKETING

Growing your business
by cultivating strategic relationships

Gerald R. Baron

OASIS PRESS
BOOKS & SOFTWARE

The Oasis Press®/PSI Research
Grants Pass, Oregon

Published by The Oasis Press®/PSI Research

This publication is designed to provide accurate and authoritative information in regard to the subject matter covered. It is sold with the understanding that the author and publisher are not engaged in rendering legal, accounting, or other professional service. If legal advice or other expert assistance is required, the ser-vices of a competent professional person should be sought.

> — from a declaration of principles jointly adopted by a committee of the American Bar Association and a committee of publishers.

Editor
Interior design by Karen K. Billipp, Eliot House Productions
Cover illustration and design by Scott Friesen/Rodney Zeiler

Please direct any comments, questions, or suggestions regarding this book to The Oasis Press®/PSI Research:

Editorial Department
300 North Valley Drive
Grants Pass, OR 97526

(541) 479-9464
(541) 476-1479 fax
psi2@magick.net e-mail

The Oasis Press® is a Registered Trademark of Publishing Services, Inc., an Oregon corporation doing business as PSI Research.

Library of Congress Cataloging-in-Publication Data

To come

Printed in the United States of America
First Edition 10 9 8 7 6 5 4 3 2 1 0
Printed on recycled paper when available

Table of Contents

Acknowledgments vi

Preview: The SALT Principles vii

Introduction: Welcome to Friendship Marketing xi
We look at three questions: How does the idea of making friends relate to business development? Is it manipulative to build friendships in the process of building your business? How can you find meaning and purpose and still build a successful business?

1: The Principles of Friendship Marketing 1
This chapter explores the underlying principles of Friendship Marketing, especially how strategic relationships affect the success of any business. It defines strategic relationships and provides examples of how these principles work in real business settings.

2: Why Listening Is So Important — and So Difficult 15
Listening is the foundation upon which friendships and business relationships are built. It is also an exceptionally difficult thing to do. Understanding why it is so difficult provides a most important clue to how Friendship Marketing really works and what it takes to make it work.

3: Two Ways to Improve Your Listening 27
A "How To" chapter that starts with the reader's personal listening skills and proceeds to explore how to build structured listening into the life of the company.

4: What Does Friendship Have to do with Anything? 43

Personal friendships and business relationships connect at certain key points but are not necessarily the same. This chapter explores the role and value of friendships in everyone's lives and then analyzes the essential elements of a business relationship.

5: The Message 59

Identifying your company's core message, however difficult, may be the most important step in effective relationship building. It requires an objective self-analysis combined with a thorough understanding of customer needs. This chapter defines the idea of the core message and identifies a process for arriving at it and effectively using it.

6: Making Friends with the Media. 77

Use of the media on one hand runs counter to the whole concept of Friendship Marketing. At the same time it is an essential part of most companies' marketing efforts. This shows when to use the media, how to choose which media are right, and how to make use of media for effectively communicating a company's core message.

7: Creating the Team 91

An essential principle of Friendship Marketing is that it is only truly effective when it is practiced by everyone in the organization. This chapter explores how to engage all levels of employees in the process of building and strengthening key relationships.

8: Selling: It Helps to Have Friends 117

The personal sales situation provides the greatest opportunity for developing key relationships and the greatest risk of abuse. This is "sales training" with service at its heart. Practical examples provide the illustrations that demonstrate building business and building relationships are not in opposition but can and should be integrated.

9: Tools: The Next Generation 137

Friendship Marketing is also an underlying principle behind the creation of effective marketing tools, including ads, brochures, public relations programs, videos, interactive media, and more. This chapter demonstrates how starting with the customers' motivations and interests drives effective graphic design and communication styles.

10: Focus: Keeping Sight of What's Important 165
Commitment to the "right few" is at the heart of this message, as it is at the heart of most business success. This chapter demonstrates why it is so hard and so important to say "no." Strategic planning is not an intellectual exercise to be accomplished by trained professionals; it is an essential element of team building requiring the involvement of everyone.

11: Don't Look for Balance at the End of this Book 183
Why balance and equilibrium in life can turn into a sad compromise. A personal journey.

Index 185

Acknowledgments

To my clients, especially those clients who are also my friends, I wish to express my sincere appreciation. Most of what I have learned is from them. This book and these ideas would not be possible if they were not generous in sharing the inner workings of their businesses and their very lives with me.

To my mother and father, I owe more than my life. They modeled for me and many others what a true partnership looks like. And they taught and demonstrated the joys and struggles of pursuing success and significance. I pass on to my readers what my parents taught me: "Enjoy the journey."

I wish to acknowledge that without the help of many people this book would not have been written or published. My clients I have already mentioned. I add to these Emmett Ramey and his staff at PSI Research/Oasis Press; my entire staff at Baron & Company, who gave me the feeling I had the freedom and responsibility to do this; and especially Robert Elmer, who gave me the professional editing and moral support I needed to actually get things done.

Finally, I wish to acknowledge my most strategic relationships: my wife and children. My children have inspired me; because of who they are I wish to become the best business person, the best writer, the best father, the best man that I can be. My wife, Lynne, has shown she believes in me even when I stop believing in myself. Without her support, encouragement, patience and confidence, I wouldn't be who I am and this book wouldn't be in your hands.

Preview

The SALT Principles

You may not want to read this book preview. It is a very concise summary of four key ideas you will find sprinkled throughout the rest of the book. If you'd rather take your time and get to the good stuff as it comes to you, I suggest getting on with Chapter 1. Then read this as a summary after you have finished the book and see if you agree that the four main ideas presented here are really what it is all about.

On the other hand, if you're in a hurry, or you'd like to see what's coming up before you make a bend in the road, or if reading the end of the book doesn't diminish your enjoyment of the book, then go ahead and read this.

Since writing this book I've been asked many times what it is about. After giving the glib "about 200 pages," I attempt to summarize the contents in a few words. This book, I tell them, is my best attempt to explain the ideas that successful companies and successful people put into practice.

It's important to note that the people behind success stories don't do what they do because someone tells them to. They succeed because these ideas work. I was most intrigued when I observed that these core ideas, time after time, contributed not only to business or career success but also toward the realization of many people's deeper desire for meaning, fulfillment and purpose.

Let me be even more concise. When forced to summarize these ideas for brief presentations such as half-day seminars, I've concluded there are four main ideas that summarize everything else:

- Strategic Relationships
- Alignment of Goals
- Listening
- Teamwork

Strategic Relationships

Effective people know how to focus their time and energies where they will do the most good. People who are looking for both success and significance have found that relationships are the integrating point in their lives. That being true, we respond two ways: 1) Focus on relationships; 2) Focus on the right, few relationships.

Can focusing on the right few result in success? I have discovered that most businesses and business people depend on far fewer key relationships than most people imagine. There is a "magic" number — a number that comes with absolute regularity in answer to the question of how many strategic relationships a person or business has.

Furthermore, I have discovered that value can be measured in relationships. The value of a business can be measured in the quality of its relationships, what they represent to the business. Even an individual's economic value — and in a certain sense, spiritual value — can be measured by the quality and nature of that person's relationships.

But who are the right few? The answer to that question is most likely found in what is really important in your life. It is a strategic question, both personally and for your business.

From a business standpoint the idea of strategic relationships is closely linked to the idea of influencers. It is most often true that a very small number of people influence all the rest. You can be strategic by knowing who the influencers are — and then influencing them.

We have chosen as a central image for "Friendship Marketing" the ripples found in still water. It is a life image as well as a business image. The impact of a point of contact at a single isolated moment causes ripples throughout a pond. In the same way, what we do now with strategic relationships — key customers, influencers, our spouses and children — will set in motion ripples of results that may be visible and experienced far into the future.

Alignment of Goals

This idea starts with the simple proposition that we are all profoundly self-centered. We live, breathe and eat largely to fulfill our own needs and desires, and we could get along quite well in this state if the rest of the world were not in the same fix. The result is a dance of competing wills, resulting in conflict, miscommunication, disappointment and failure. Most problems with relationships, including important customer relationships, are caused by this competition of needs.

The solution? I'm suggesting that when you are motivated to build a long-term, loyal, trusting relationship, it falls on you to start the process. What will occur resembles what naturally occurs in friendships. There is a moment of discovery when two people who are about to become friends find that they hold something in common, something important to both of them.

However, friendship is not the desired end of all business relationships, but a model to understand. If we do understand, we will better know how to develop the kinds of relationships we are looking for. And it starts with an alignment of goals.

Listening

If alignment of goals is the "secret" that makes building strong relationships possible or even easy, then listening is the hard work needed to make it happen. While this kind of listening is extremely difficult, it is also very powerful.

Listening is difficult and powerful for the very reason why relationships are troublesome and alignment of goals so important. We are more interested in ourselves, our ideas and our objectives than anyone else's. When you listen, however, you turn this fact to your advantage, because the person to whom you are listening is just like you: self-centered. They are more interested in their ideas, their needs and their hopes than they are in yours. By demonstrating sincere interest in what is important to others, things change.

What changes is that you have knowledge, knowledge of the important things on which your relationships can be based. What also changes is respect. By listening, you have demonstrated respect and the wisdom of recognizing the value of what the other person is saying. By listening, the basis for a trusting relationship is laid.

Teamwork

I have come to call teamwork the "Power and the Glory." I use the term the "Power," because in a company setting, the work of building the business cannot be accomplished without cooperation from the rest of the team. When building a relationship, all the good one person or group can do can be quickly destroyed if others don't understand the importance of that relationship, or if they aren't equally committed to developing the relationship. But when the team gets together, when they have one shining goal in front of them, when they share the challenge equally, there is great power.

Teamwork is also called "the Glory" because operating as part of an effective team is its own reward. Most people crave the experience of being part of a truly effective team, working in concert to accomplish something that individuals could not do. The trophy may be held high, but for years we remember with fondness the joy of celebration, the experience of pulling together, the warmth of knowing others were covering for you in your weaknesses and that you covered for others.

With this in view, every manager is responsible for setting the challenges high. If for no other reason, setting high goals gives the team an opportunity to come together and to experience the glory of teamwork.

Strategic relationships, alignment of goals, listening and teamwork spell more than a clever acronym. Taken together, they promise to help you combine ideas that work and a road to deeper purpose. My hope is that these SALT principles can change the way you do business, and in the process serve as a flavorful seasoning for the business of life.

> *"Friendship is always a sweet responsibility,*
> *never an opportunity."*
> — **Kahlil Gibran**

Introduction

Welcome to Friendship Marketing

This book is about a remarkably simple concept: making friends. You're going to discover that the business of business is making friends and the role of managers and employees is to make friends. Even beyond business, our lives would all be richer if we spent more time building friendships.

No one questions that making friends is a good thing. But one question will immediately strike those with a high degree of ethical sensitivity. How can we suggest that business success comes through friendships? Isn't that manipulative?

The cynical reader will find much of use here, but that would be looking from the wrong end of the telescope. At heart, this book is more about successful living than business success, and yet these are not two ends of the spectrum. They are not even competing forces that need to be balanced. I learned that lesson from the owner of a local coffee shop.

A lesson from a busy entrepreneur.

She was a woman a little older than my wife, Lynne, with a husband and three nearly grown daughters. She poured heart and soul into her little enterprise, working horribly long hours and fighting through all the struggles of getting her business off the ground.

As they got to be better friends, Lynne talked with her through serious difficulties in her life, difficulties that would discourage almost anyone. Then a tragedy of unimaginable proportions struck.

The woman's oldest daughter, a young mother, was killed in a horrifying accident at home. When Lynne and I went to her funeral, my first thought was how unimportant that coffee shop must seem to Lynne's friend at that time. Considering all the struggles in her life, and this horrific blow, I mused whether she regretted having poured all that energy of her life into that little business.

But then I looked around and I saw 600 people trying to crowd into a church built for 400. I saw the expressions of love and support that this woman received. And I knew that so many of those people, like my wife, became her close friends because they were her customers at her little coffee shop. If you could measure worth and value in effort, this was it.

The true worth of her business wasn't the money she made or could have made. It was the friends and loving relationships that she developed in the course of the two or three years that she had the shop.

Was she in business to make money? Certainly. But the money meant little or nothing in that time of deep sorrow. The friends, on the other hand, meant everything. When I realized this, it put business and the reasons for being in business in a whole new light.

Choose a focus.

Maybe being in business or working at your job is the best means you have of meeting interesting people, people with the potential to become friends who can contribute more to your life than money ever can. Looked at in this way, the message of this book can be "Develop Business," because in the process of developing business you will make friends who will contribute to your life in immeasurable ways. The message of this book could also be "Make Friends," because in the process of doing that in your business life you will build the basis for long-term career success.

Keep it simple.

I'm certain that every entrepreneur and every executive has felt totally confused at one time or another, and it's possible that many of us spend a good part of our time in confusion. That's when a simple little idea like "Make Friends" can really help.

I can say to myself, "I may not make all these decisions correctly, and I may screw up more than I care to admit. But I know that if I concentrate on doing what I need to do for my friends or if I develop the friendships that are important to me, I'll be okay."

That idea can clear a tremendous amount of clutter off the busy desk of your mind. If this book helps accomplish that, I will have succeeded.

— Gerald R. Baron
Bellingham, Washington

"The happiest business in all the
world is making friends."
— Austin O'Malley

1

The Principles of Friendship Marketing

Strategic relationships will make or break any business, no matter how big, no matter what kind of market. But what are they, exactly? This chapter explains how relationships work in real business settings by outlining the basic principles of Friendship Marketing. But first, a word about what really drives business...

Chapter summary:

- Is business really "Me First?"
- Feed me, Seymour!
- Discovering the personal angle.
- The real equity of a business is found in its relationships.
- Tomorrow's business depends on today's relationships.
- Most businesses depend on far fewer relationships than they realize.
- Change your future by strengthening, changing or adding relationships.
- Discover new business in existing relationships.
- Look to the leaders.
- Relationship building is a team effort.
- The real bottom line.

I suddenly had this rather frightening thought. It is very clear that we live in a time when self-adulation has reached historic proportions. Self-fulfillment, self-assertiveness, personal rights, personal choice — all these have become sacred duties.

The result of this thinking is increasingly obvious in how people behave toward each other or what kind of service you get when you go to a store or a restaurant. Business, more than anything else, appears to fly highest when driven by the insatiable desire for self-fulfillment and personal satisfaction. At least, that's the common perception: that business is driven by the prospect of all the toys we can buy to satisfy our deepest needs.

Is business really "Me First"?

Business may have a bad reputation for self-centered greed, but in my experience, business people succeed for the same reasons as everyone else: They are willing to sacrifice their own narrow self-interest to meet the needs of another. Businesses succeed when they focus their energies on serving those people who have an interest in what they are providing. Giving, not pure getting, works in business.

Here's the scary part. Suppose all those young people growing up in our culture and in front of today's television sets finally enter the work world and discover that it's not really so. Suppose they find out that the way to get ahead is not by stepping on everyone around; that single-minded pursuit of what's good for me isn't what works in the workplace; that to get you have to give. And worse, if you give to get, it's not really giving.

Or, what would happen if all those people never really learned?

What if they all reported to work carrying only their "Me first" attitudes? I can't begin to imagine the horrors coming out the engineering departments; the managers screaming about why they can't get what they want out of anybody; the marketers all screaming louder than one another about what THEY really love about their products — and no one else paying any attention.

Business would grind to a halt and shrivel into chaos. Everyone would finally be so busy chasing the elusive WIIFM ("What's in it for Me") that no transactions would occur. And just like in the movies, we would get a full taste of the dark side of human nature.

Feed me, Seymour!

The huge houseplant in the entertaining musical "Little Shop of Horrors" comes to life and begs its friend to feed him. "Feed me, Seymour," it begins to plead.

At first, the plant's requests are plaintive, almost pitiful. Then it becomes more and more persistent: "Feed me, Seymour, feed me!"

Seymour becomes frantic in his efforts to meet the demands, but the harder he tries, the more demanding the plant becomes. "Feed me! Feed me! Feed me!" Even when Seymour feeds a lecherous dentist to Seymour it is not enough, and finally the insatiable plant tries to feed on Seymour himself.

It is comic, fascinating, horrifying theater. It's also a great picture of the customer, and that includes all of us at some time. We're insatiable in our desires to be entertained, to be fed, to be served, to be taken care of. And the more service we get, the more we want.

We want fast parcel delivery. Pick up at 4 P.M. and guaranteed delivery the next day by 10:30 A.M. Then, once we receive that kind of service, we look for someone else who will deliver by 9 A.M. Or even same-day delivery, if possible.

Eventually even a courier isn't fast enough. Fax it. Get it there almost instantly. And if it gets there almost instantly we become impatient standing by the fax machine while it takes several long moments calling up another name, then literally minutes to send all the pages across town or across the world. For some of us, even a fax is too slow.

In the same way, we want lower prices. So discounters build big warehouses and stack groceries up to the ceilings and send all the workers home, including almost all the cashiers. That done, we have to stand in line for ten or fifteen minutes. And while we're standing there we're thinking, "This is ridiculous. The prices are great, now, but why can't these people hire enough employees to take care of me?"

"Feed me, Seymour. Feed me!"

Let's talk entertainment for a moment. I'm afraid to admit I can remember where one black-and-white channel on the television, filled with snow and all, was an unbelievable treat. With "The Wonderful World of Disney" and Jack Smith's "You Asked For It," what else did anyone need?

Now we have 30-something channels with 500 promised soon. Still we shuttle desperately back and forth between the house, video store and movie theater because there's nothing good on the tube.

"Feed me! Feed me! Feed ME NOW!"

Discovering the personal angle.

We're an insatiable lot. But this isn't a book about social criticism and what's gone wrong with our society. This is an appeal to business owners and managers to understand the appetite, because from a business perspective, appetite equals opportunity. And insatiable appetite equals unlimited opportunity.

Understand this, if nothing else: The more needs there are in the world, the more opportunities you have to fill them. And the greater the intensity of the need, the greater the opportunity to become the hero, the friend who satisfies them. This is no "Little Shop of Horrors" with a plant that will nibble on your leg. This is nothing less than a ticket to business success.

However, there's a difference between understanding the principles and putting them to work in your own business. As we find out how it's done, resist the temptation to translate concepts into formulas.

I have always resisted the idea that business was about numbers, even though numbers are important. So beware: We may be duped into thinking the bottom line is all about numbers when we look at the world of mega-companies and mega-deals.

Look behind all the high finance and you'll find real people meeting the needs of other real people. The big investment bankers may be moving money from one computerized cyber location to another, thinking they have accomplished something. But whether they are dealing with oil or pork futures, business still comes down to basic things like someone pumping oil out of the ground and someone else selling it to a customer. Pork still comes from someone feeding piglets (albeit by push button) and someone else selling bacon to a supermarket chain buyer.

Perhaps I will eventually come across a business that doesn't include personal transactions. If I do, I'm afraid it won't be very interesting. In the meantime, business still ultimately boils down to people dealing with people. Even in the technology-centered world we live in, that's what it's all about. And that's the big idea behind the following seven principles.

The real equity of a business is found in its relationships.

Business commentator Peter Drucker has said that profits are merely the right to do business in the future. He's very right, but the thought should be carried one step further. Positive relationships between your company and your customers are the foundation on which your future business is built. And if that is true, then it is ultimately good relationships that give you the opportunity to do business in the future.

On the other hand, poor relationships pull your business into a big hole, just as certainly as deficit spending or a lack of profits. Digging out is no easy task.

You might look at the value of your company from a real estate perspective. When it's time to sell a business, accountants and lawyers come in to say what the operation is worth. Value is usually based on profits or asset value. Even goodwill, when considered, is intangible and formulaic.

But neither profits nor assets can define the value of a business apart from its relationships. For example, profits are only one proof that you have positive customer relationships. You might say that since people are buying your products, their acceptance represents value. That's close, but not quite. That kind of thinking is deceptive.

I've seen clever advertising succeed in convincing people that there is more value to a product or service than can be supported by its quality. Sooner or later (probably sooner) the word gets out, the reputation takes a nose dive, sales dry up and so do profits. Profits then, were illusory, supported not by solid relationships but by short-lived deception.

What about hard assets? Surely things like your office copier, the facilities or manufacturing equipment are valuable apart from relationships. You know the price tags.

But if someone buys your equipment at auction to start a business just like yours, you can guess what it will be used for — developing new customers. Think of it for a moment. The only value in those assets is their potential to be used in developing solid customer relationships.

That's it. If you couldn't use your desks or office equipment to create and satisfy customers, then they are only good for someone else for the same purpose.

Viewing your business this way may very well change the emphasis you place on your personal activities. It may take some of your attention off production efficiencies, or always trying to get the cost per unit down to the lowest possible number. It may make you reevaluate the time spent on preparing the slickest presentations for bankers or investors.

Of course, I'm not suggesting that those kinds of activities aren't important. But when you recognize where your true business value is, you can shift priorities and delegate lower priorities to others. Job number one is taking care of your customers.

Tomorrow's business depends on today's relationships.

Here's the closest I come to a crystal ball prediction. If you want to know how sales are going to be in the future, take a good look at existing customer relationships.

Look at your business from their perspective. Sometimes that requires a bit of market research, to understand how satisfied your customers (and ex-customers) are with quality, price, service or delivery. Of course, it's more complicated than that because you need to factor in the competition, as well.

For instance, a retailer may be doing an abysmal job of taking care of customers but still manage to do reasonably well because the competition is doing even worse. If customers translate this into a high degree of satisfaction, good for the retailer. They're one of the lucky few. But this retailer had better keep a close eye out for a new competitor. Make sure you're not in this position. I guarantee that eventually someone will emerge who's smarter and has done his or her homework to discover a ripe market opportunity.

Most businesses depend on far fewer relationships than they realize.

When it occurred to me that relationships were at the core of every business, I started asking seminar attendees this simple question: "How many business relationships do you have that your business truly depends on?" How many people do you know who play key roles in determining important future business?

I had already come up with an arbitrary number during early conversations with clients. Most businesses, I reasoned, would certainly be able to identify 15 important, dependent relationships. But soon I was startled to discover a much lower number. Many business executives could only identify between five and seven key, critical outside relationships!

The size of business didn't matter. Executives with companies doing more than $100 million in annual sales often identified fewer key relationships than staff from many of the startup companies.

There are exceptions. I tried the question on a supermarket chain client, expecting to find out about far more than five customers. After all, they had five stores, some with volumes of over a half million dollars in sales and 35,000 customers per week.

The leadership of this supermarket chain could identify quite a number of key relationships. But when we analyzed existing market research data I was surprised to find that a relatively small percentage did the majority of the business. Even for a business as dispersed in customers as a discount supermarket, the basic principle held true: A relatively small number of relationships are absolutely crucial to the business.

If you discover this principle you also discover the important result: You don't have to reach very many people to impact your business. In fact, in one seminar I offered my audience what I consider to be the world's simplest (and most effective) marketing plan. Actually, it's the next principle.

Change your future by strengthening, changing or adding relationships.

The idea is so simple, yet so powerful. Simply find the people that will mean to your business what your critical relationships mean to you now. Then make them your friends.

That's it. Just go find them. Make them your friends. Here's how it works in practice.

Let's say your company currently has customers all over the U.S., Canada and Mexico. You want to expand your business by 50 percent. The thought of doing that may be daunting. You're thinking, I'll have to roll out a big promotion campaign, add to my sales staff, put out a big mailing. Big bucks. Then you read this book and decide to take a good hard look at where your current business is coming from.

You find that about 80 percent of the business comes from about 20 percent of your customers. In my experience I've found that the ratio is more like 90/10. So instead of having one thousand customers, you find that most of the business is coming from the top twenty. In fact, in that top twenty there are only a handful, say five, that are consistently ordering more than anyone else.

Then it strikes you. To increase my business 50 percent I don't need to find 500 new customers. I only have to find another five who will do the same amount of business those top five are doing.

Finding five good customers from all across North America couldn't be that hard, could it?

With those kinds of numbers and that kind of focus it isn't hard to see that you can change your business in a hurry just by changing new relationships. Adding just a few new key customers can make a huge difference, if they are the right ones for you.

Look carefully, though. This principle doesn't say that "adding" is the only way to change your future business. It said "strengthening" and "changing," as well. And I'll prove to you that you can increase your business fifty percent without adding a single new relationship. That would be even easier, but to do that you have to buy into the next principle.

Discover new business in existing relationships.

Amazing, but true. It's long been said that the cost of keeping a customer is much less than the cost of gaining a new one. I never could figure out how they came up with the math on that so I'm not going to try to work it out. But we're not just talking about keeping a customer, we're talking about getting additional business from that customer. We're talking about building your business by increasing the value your customer places on his or her relationship to you.

You can look at this several ways. Perhaps you sell car parts to small repair shops. A limited number of cars break down, however, so the shops only need a limited number of parts. How can you increase that?

First, think of the other items your customers need that you are not now carrying. Things like a new soap to clean the grease off their hands or a new car wax they could sell to their customers. You could even sell the shop owner one of those purple and blue neon "OPEN" signs. Use your imagination.

And that's just the start. Try increasing your value to those you supply by helping them increase their business. Say a shop owner buys some of his parts from you and some from your competitors. If you're talking to him about his business, give him a great idea or two about how to increase his volume or his productivity. At the same time, let him know how much you're interested in doing more business with him. As a result, you could see your orders increase.

Keep in mind that companies often get stuck in a rut of perception that locks in who they are and how their customers think of them. Limit your thinking about who you are to your customers, and you limit your opportunities with that customer. It's as simple as that.

For example, a small accounting firm may be in the business of putting out financial statements for a small group of key clients. Then by looking at the numbers, the head of the firm notices some trends. She realizes that the client could increase his or her cash flow by liquidating many of the older, inactive assets.

Maybe I should mention it, she wonders, but quickly decides against saying anything. I'm not paid to be a consultant, she tells herself. My job is to do their financial statements.

That's limiting. Instead, the accountant could take the client to lunch and tell him that she can help by doing an in-depth financial analysis, including ways to improve the bottom line.

"I've looked at your situation," she could tell the client, "and here's one idea I'd like to throw at you ...."

The client is amazed, overwhelmed and extremely grateful, so the accountant quickly adds that "this is just one simple idea. I'm confident there is much more I could find by spending a little more time. I think maybe ten to twenty hours would get us a good start, and by the way, I charge $250 an hour for this management consulting service."

Now this accountant isn't just the one who puts out the P & L. Not any more. She's turned into a friend who's going to help improve her client's business. And because the client now thinks of her as a well-paid management consultant, he positively expects her to drive off in a Porsche — and pick up the lunch tab.

Look to the leaders.

Listen in on a discussion between two generals. They face a well-armed, well-entrenched enemy. One general says, "We can take them straight on. Yes, it will be a bloody day, but war is hell."

The other general says, "I have a confirmed intelligence report that says they have carelessly placed all their ammunition and food in one location. We can blow this up and then let them shoot until they have no food or ammo left."

Which general is being strategic?

Being strategic is simply finding the quickest, easiest, least expensive and most effective way to get to your destination. We understand that concept almost instinctively, yet it continually amazes me how many people resist the idea of saving themselves time, effort and money.

Consider the consistent findings of communication research, which tells us over and again that approximately 10 percent of any group, population or industry are the real opinion leaders. These are the people that others look to for guidance.

The customers you want will follow their own opinion leaders, as well. You benefit by establishing good relationships with those leaders, because where they go, others will follow.

Look at it this way: Apple Computer early on identified that computer buyers would learn much about computers in schools. They established strategic relationships with the schools, even donating thousands of new computers to education. Or a proprietor of a high class restaurant understands that if the town's wealthiest and most sophisticated people are seen at her establishment, it will influence others who wish to be like them.

That's what I mean by suggesting that some relationships are strategic. Others will look at you and make judgments about your business based on who your customers are. The more respect they have for those customers, the more respect you gain.

Knowing that, if you wish to develop business within a targeted group, the smart thing — the strategic thing — is to focus your attention on those people the others respect. Do this because not all relationships are of equal value.

Somehow that sounds cold and calculated, and this is where the entire relationship concept clearly gets a little dicey. I don't mean to say for an instant that relationships are important only because of what they can do for you. Personal relationships will always have a value far beyond business.

In addition, anyone who treats people as objects for pure gain will soon be identified as a shallow fraud and will deservedly be left friendless on and off the job. We'll learn more about this in Chapter 4.

None of that contradicts the truth that not all business relationships are of equal value. Advertising icon David Ogilvy said that the customer is always right until he repeatedly asks you to lose business on his account. If that's his idea of fairness and you can't change it, you had better move on.

I have found more than once that no matter how hard I tried, I just could not please some people. I don't know why, some people seem to be happiest being unhappy. Then, of course, there are those who had a right to be upset with me and I was never able to fully make it up to them. For whatever reason, if you have tried and tried and you still can't make a business relationship happy, by all means leave it behind to focus on the ones you can make happy.

This principle is true for more than just service businesses. If someone thinks they can get equal or better quality at a better price somewhere else, but you know your quality is better and you can't or won't lower your price, you're never going to make them happy. Why try?

Instead, you need to find those who understand and value the quality you are selling. They will find your price perfectly reasonable, and those are the people you can make happy. Never concern yourself too much with the others.

If you follow this philosophy, you'll be helping the right people place a high value on what you do. In that case, there is such a thing as "right" people and therefore there are also "wrong" people. Concentrate on the right people and chances are everyone will be happy.

Unfortunately, even if you're sold on this idea about making friends to build your business, reality is always a little more complicated than you hope for. Let's say you've told your new customer/friend that understanding and caring for his needs are important to you. You promise him that you are going to do what it takes, and you mean it.

The next day, though, the customer calls your office to make an appointment to discuss a large order with you, and disaster strikes quietly. The receptionist treats him like he's another one of those obnoxious stock broker telemarketers and fails to get you the message.

You routinely call on him a few days later and he let's you know what he thinks of your service. Somehow, however, you get it all straightened out by apologizing profusely and he places a small order to give you a try.

Next you check with production and they tell you next Wednesday for delivery. You pass on that timeline to the client with assurances you'll come through for him.

Friday comes and you're frantic. The production manager calmly explains that another customer got priority and bumped your schedule since "it was just a small order for a new client."

You're furious and go back to the client to try to convince him you were serious about taking care of him. By that time it's far too late, though, which leads us to the next principle.

Relationship building is a team effort.

Look at every business as a relationship-building team. It's not a one-person job. That's why these concepts are so important if you're a business owner or top executive who can do something about building an entire relationship-building system.

The fact is, though, that everyone from the delivery person to the chairman of the board needs to be involved in relationship building. Our best efforts to build relationships can be short circuited at any point along the way through the lengthy process of marketing, selling, producing, delivering, collecting, and checking satisfaction.

One of the main challenges facing entrepreneurs and business executives today is showing everyone in their organization the vital role they play in the company's efforts to build long-lasting customer friendships. Retail executives, for example, spend endless hours figuring out how to buy products better, how to improve merchandising, how to maximize sales and how to advertise. Yet not all of them fully realize that all this good work can go to waste because of what happens in a moment at the checkstand.

A recent national poll showed that grocery store checkout clerks were considered the second-worst service personnel in American business. How can this be? They are the culmination of everyone else's hard work, then they're somehow allowed the opportunity to be surly and unresponsive. It's unimaginable!

How much value would be added to many of the country's biggest retail giants if they would only excel at hiring and keeping people in the checkstand who made every customer feel great.

The real bottom line.

Before we move on to consider how these principles apply to every aspect of marketing, let's make sure we understand what's working against us from the start. We may understand the concepts well enough, but a common inclination will sabotage all our efforts at success in personal relationships, in marketing, or in business performance.

The problem is inescapable. Even if we buy into many of the concepts presented in this book, we will have difficulty implementing them simply because of selfishness.

How incredibly old-fashioned it seems, yet not as old-fashioned as the theological concept that predates it: original sin. According to the Genesis account, God wanted people to be oriented in thought, action and purpose to Him. Trouble is, people from the beginning have misused their divinely granted freedom to pursue their own course. The results, unfortunately, have proven to be disastrous.

It would be fun to debate the merits of that ancient idea here. Instead, let's find out whether we really are so intensely self-oriented, and whether this could be an explanation for the difficulty we all have focusing on relationships.

Social Darwinists agree that we are intensely self-interested, reasoning that self-interest is the truest course to survival in a competitive world. Free enterprise advocates add that enlightened self-interest makes the market system truly efficient and effective. Neither philosophy will argue against the idea of selfishness, though they may argue with my suggestion that selfishness prevents the person and the business from achieving its true potential.

Who's left to argue? Today's "good" people who know right from wrong and generally choose to pursue the right, who understand that unselfishness is sometimes difficult but usually quite possible. They acknowledge that personal and corporate self-centeredness may sometimes interfere with relationship building. Yet they doubt selfishness has the depth, strength and persistence to prevent action to the degree I am suggesting. These people (and there's a very good chance that they include you) are going to be tough to convince. I will offer only one example as evidence: a baby.

I've had the very great privilege of raising three of my own, as well as observing numerous nieces and nephews. Especially to their parents, all were as cute, darling and precious as an infant can be.

Yet no one who has really watched a baby can question the fact that they live totally, completely and innocently for themselves alone. Every waking moment is lived for the purpose of filling needs — their needs. They call for food, for entertainment, for comfort, for a clean diaper, for warmth.

There is absolutely no give in an infant, in whom the love is purely one-sided. The smile that warms a parent's heart can be seen as a gift, and it certainly is taken as such by most admirers. Yet the smile involves no sacrifice or willful overcoming of selfish impulses.

Then comes a magic time when the toddler or young child makes a gesture of unselfishness. It may be when another infant cries. The youngster may look at her bottle, look over at the crying younger brother, and decide to offer it to him. It is a thoughtful moment. The cost is weighed. Perhaps due to the example of a parent, that young child makes a decision to forgo pleasure and personal need for the sake of someone else.

Such unselfishness signals the end of infancy. Suddenly, this is someone with whom a human relationship is possible, for the simple reason that she demonstrates a willingness to overcome the natural and powerful bent toward self-fulfillment.

Surely we see examples all around us of those who "pass the bottle." If you are ever lucky enough to observe such a sight it may fill you with wonder, which in itself proves that we know how difficult it is to overcome self-serving instincts.

At the same time, it's quite possible to get something valuable out of this book without subscribing to the idea of innate self-centeredness and the problems that it leads to. But if you wonder why you're having a tough time implementing the ideas that make sense to you, look first to this cause.

"If A equals success, the formula is A equals X plus
Y and Z, with X being work, Y play and Z
keeping your mouth shut."
— Albert Einstein

2

Why Listening Is So Important — and So Difficult

Look at a drawing of one person listening and one person talking. Which one is the friend? Most would say the listener. To improve your friendships, you learn how to listen better. To enrich your marriage, you cultivate the fine art of listening.

It's not so strange, then, that better listening is the key to developing the success of any business. Your business. But there's a right way — and a wrong way.

Chapter summary:

- Just give me a paper!
- When the gift of gab isn't.
  - Listening makes you a friend.
  - Listening makes you look smart.
  - Listening actually makes you smart.
- Why listening is so hard.
  - Listening is hard because it's more fun to talk.
  - Listening is hard because self-interest gets in the way.
  - Listening is hard because it's not passive.
  - Listening is hard because our brains crave action.
  - Listening is hard because it takes precious time.

The subject of listening seems foreign to most of us in business. What does listening have to do with it? We're all about profits and sales and efficiencies. Who has time to listen?

Apparently, the most successful companies in the country have time. Or they find it. The best have developed a keen interest in what their customers and other important people think about them. They listen, and then they respond.

On the other hand, struggling companies often share a sense of confusion about what others are thinking about them. Sometimes you even see an attitude that says, "I don't much care what they think; after all, we've been doing this for a long time and we know a lot more about these things than they do."

That's a real shame, because if relationships are the bedrock of business success, listening is the essential foundation on which relationships are built. I hope I can make that very clear. Listening is the foundation, the only certain way to build long-term business success. If you don't listen, you won't succeed. Simple as that.

Even though this message is coming at all of us from every direction, I am continually amazed at how difficult it is for business people to take serious listening seriously. Even many marketing experts, who should understand the principle, miss abundant opportunities to build business success through listening. They allow so many other things to get in the way.

Just give me a paper!

For months I intended to order a newspaper subscription at home, but never thought of calling to order at the right time. I might remember it on a lazy Sunday morning as I was on my way to the convenience store to pick one up, but of course I couldn't call the subscription department then. (By the way, why are these service businesses only open when everyone else is at work, and then closed when you have time to think about dealing with them?)

Finally I happened to be out on the street when the paper boy came by. *Great*, I thought. *I can ask him. He'd be happy to get the new business.* But he said no, I'd have to call the office if I wanted a subscription.

I'm sure the paper boy had his reasons. It might have even been paper policy. But couldn't he have offered to call the subscription department for me, or taken my name and sent it in? And would they not then be impressed with his business development skills?

Maybe he doesn't get paid by the number of customers on his route. If not, what a mistake. Or maybe he is seen to be at the bottom of the newspaper totem pole.

He's just the delivery person. But what they don't understand is that this young boy is the one most likely to meet the paper's reading customers on a regular basis. He is the one who puts the face on the paper. His ears are closest to the people who really matter — the readers.

Unfortunately, this paper's management has communicated to this young man that his ears are unimportant. It is only his legs on the bike and his arms flinging the papers onto the front steps or stuffing them into the boxes that counts. So they are missing opportunities. In my case, a mere $12 per month, but how many more like me are out there?

More importantly, the fact that the newspaper's management did not work with their young carriers on service and listening is obvious in other areas of the operation. Their sales staff reflects the same attitude; even their reporters and editors communicate in a variety of ways that they have little concern for the sensitivity and values of the community they serve. Listening, it turns out, is an attitude that can permeate an organization. And if it is visibly missing in one element of the enterprise, there's a good chance it is missing throughout the entire operation.

When the gift of gab isn't.

What's your image of a good sales person? What's his or her most important tool? I like to ask these questions in my seminars, and the answer is predictable.

Sure. The mouth. That's everyone's stereotype. The big toothy smile, the ingratiating style and the high-energy, non-stop patter that finally drives the victim insane.

But the correct answer is, of course, the ears. The best sales people I've ever seen have sold by asking questions. I once watched in amazement as an IBM salesman sold a $100,000 computer to a friend. The meeting was pleasant, but the salesman was far from pushy. Despite the enormous price tag of the item, he didn't need to be. He simply asked questions and listened to the answers.

Here's why listening is so important:

Listening makes you a friend.

Listening is a fundamental friendship skill. It's the way all of us establish bonds of affection, caring and mutual understanding. And more than that, listening has a way of turning enemies into friends.

Almost like magic, listening can turn a heated controversy into understanding. In business, listening is the best opportunity to turn a legitimately angry customer into a loyal friend. Next time you're in a customer service line, preferably right after a major buying holiday like Christmas, watch for the real pros behind the counter. They're the ones who turn upset customers into loyal friends. They're the listeners.

If we took that one little lesson to heart, our businesses would see dramatic improvements, our working relationships on the job would flourish, and our families would think we'd completely lost our marbles.

If you're still not sure how important listening is, visit a bookstore and try scanning the titles on marriage or how to improve relationships. Look for the word "communication" in any of the titles or book jackets, and you'll see what I mean. The good books will give advice on how to listen. The others focus on how to talk, which is really tricking the other person into listening when they can't or don't want to.

Listening and relationship building are so closely linked because listening is really a direct, tangible form of caring. Listening confirms that you value a customer or a client as a person, that you care for them, accept them, respect them. Remember, their words are the most personal, most direct, most tangible expression of who they really are.

So beware. Toss their words away with a bored look, an interruption or a glance at your watch and you send a clear message that cannot be retracted: I don't care much about you.

The key thing to remember about listening is often the toughest thing for driving, results-oriented business people to grasp. Listen to learn, but don't stop there. Listen to demonstrate that you are listening. The act of listening in itself is almost more important than what you hear.

Listening makes you look smart.

"Better to remain silent and be thought a fool than to open one's mouth and remove all doubt." Mark Twain may not have said that, but it sounds like him. The funny thing is, if you do keep your mouth shut, the other person is likely to think you're a genius.

It's really quite simple. Since many of us are convinced that what we have to say is the wisest and most important thing that can be said, a person who genuinely listens to us gives the impression that he or she also values what we say.

As usual, the concept applies directly to business, and I have adopted a listener's rule of thumb about a first meeting with a prospective client. I resolve to talk no more than 20 percent of the time, leaving the other 80 percent to listen.

One of the reasons, of course, is to gain useful information that I will need to make a meaningful proposal. But more importantly, I want the other person to think I am smart. The best way I can convince them is by listening.

Think back to just about any recent conversation you've had. Maybe you were talking with your spouse about a conversation you had that day with a difficult person. Your spouse, being interested, asks, "What did he say?"

At first you might answer his or her question. But invariably you tell what you said in the conversation, and the detail of your response comes flooding back to you in glorious and even embellished specifics.

"So I told him..." you recount, forgetting that the question was about what they said to you, not what you said to them. It's amazing how easy it is to recall our own part of conversations and difficult to recall the other person's contributions. And of course, our contributions tend to grow in value as they are remembered and recounted to others.

Consider business conversation in those terms. If you want prospective new clients to think back positively on your initial meeting, the best way is for them to recall all the smart things they said to you. You can help that process along by listening.

Asking questions is a part of listening as well. To find out more about a company I like to ask questions such as, "Where do you see your business going in five years?" or "Do you see the current fluctuations in the dollar affecting you?" Then I sit back to listen or take notes.

Asking questions not only makes you look pretty sharp without committing yourself to any position, it gives others the floor to show you their vision, their experience, and their ability to address business leadership questions. Later, they will remember the depth of your conversation and what they said to you. Listening, which includes asking the right questions, makes you look very smart. Listening also makes them feel smart.

Listening actually makes you smart.

Listening helps turn you into a friend, and listening makes you look smart. But fortunately, there's much more to listening than appearances. People who listen not only look smart, they really are smart. Now we go beyond the meaning of the act of listening to listening as a way to gain useful information.

Think of it this way. Your customers own all the information you need to make your business a success. The answer to virtually any question rests with them. The right path in your strategic plan can be determined by listening to your customers. The features you need to build into your next product or model upgrade can be identified by listening to your customers.

They have the information that will make you smart. All it takes is the discipline and exercise of listening to them. As we'll find out, however, that may be easier said than done.

Why listening is so hard.

Even though listening is important and its benefits are enormous, listening is still a rare art because it's just plain hard work.

I can think of at least five reasons why. Fortunately, there are ways to get around each one.

Listening is hard because it's more fun to talk.

I've met very few people who like to listen. In fact, many of us have the idea that what we have to say is much more valuable than what nearly anyone else has to say.

"Well, of course," you might be thinking. "That's because the people I have to listen to are real dunderheads. If there was someone who really had something to say it would be different."

I suggest that if we met the President or the Prime Minister or a top business executive we might initially be awed into silence. After awhile, though, most of us might express an opinion or two. Then, if the awesome personality listened to us, we might start to believe our opinion was pretty significant. Given time, we could easily come to believe that our opinion was in some cases even better than the celebrity's.

Our culture and the media compound the problem, telling us in a thousand subtle ways that successful people, those with power and authority, don't listen. They talk. See a politician on television, and they're talking. Celebrities talk while everybody else watches. If you work for a big company and you see the president, chances are he or she is speaking, too.

Be careful not to apply this concept to your business. Don't trust your instinct if it tells you to talk a lot, listen a little. Just the opposite is true.

So listen closely. Maybe the "talk first" philosophy has already taken hold in your company. To see if it has, try this: Count all the time your company spends preparing, planning, organizing and creating "messages" that the company will send out to the public — things like press releases, advertising and public statements. Compare it to the time spent listening to the customers. If your company is like most, talk time far overshadows listening time.

That's the unfortunate part. For most people drawn to marketing, listening is hardly the main attraction. They got into selling because they "enjoy people" so much, which usually means they like to talk a lot. Or they went into marketing because it offered some opportunity for creative expression, which means they like to let others know what they are thinking. In either case, the boat is being missed.

Listening may not be as much fun, but we'll never turn our businesses around unless we start treating listening as the prime marketing skill.

Listening is hard because self-interest gets in the way.

What makes listening so hard? Plain and simple self-interest. If we had the same interest in others as we had in ourselves, listening would not be a painful obligation. It would be a joy. And if businesses want to truly serve the interests of their customers, they will find listening a natural, essential and most enjoyable part of their everyday function.

Think back again to our earlier discussion about self-centeredness and babies. Without exception, all of us are absorbed with our needs, our ideas, our contributions, our image, our satisfaction. It is an absolutely fundamental aspect of humanity and anyone who thinks otherwise, such as Karl Marx, will ultimately be embarrassed. My own suspicion is that Marx probably never understood babies, or at least never got close enough to see how impossible social utopia really is, given the way we really are.

Teenagers are another example of that self-centeredness, when the infant tendency returns with a vengeance unexpected by most parents. As one teenager told her incredulous father, "You seem to have forgotten that the operative word here is 'ME!' "

Sadly, she's right. For babies, teenagers and adults, extreme self-interest can inflate to the point where there is no interest left in the other person. Self-interest says, "I am a good and valuable person and I have a right to pursue my own needs, wants and satisfaction." Self-interest may even go so far as to say, "My need to hear myself talk is more important to me than your need to hear yourself talk."

The problem is, modern psychobabble encourages the extreme pursuit of self-interest. On television and radio talk shows we hear that the only way to peace, satisfaction and good living is by giving yourself permission to have interest only in you. Certainly there are people with shriveled self-images who need to be built up, but the relentless pursuit of selfishness is not the way to do it.

A sort of balance is illustrated in our free enterprise market system. This is the system that has been fabulously successful in creating both wealth and a competitive environment that benefits consumers. That's because capitalism is based on the simple idea that we all tend to pursue our own wants, needs and satisfactions.

Self-interest drives the consumer economy, but it also trips up unsuspecting businesses that lose track of the bigger picture. When a company becomes too self-engrossed in its own agenda, it forgets that the customers, those people it exists for, are really only interested in the magic WIIFM: "What's In It For Me."

Here's the dilemma. If business persons are only interested in WIIFM, they might be completely concerned with things like maximizing profits, minimizing costs and saving up for retirement. On the other hand, the customer may only be interested in WIIFM as well, in issues like getting the highest quality with the greatest degree of convenience, and personal service at the lowest possible cost.

If there is no area in which those two WIIFM's meet, then it's up to the competition to demonstrate some interest in the customer's WIIFM and take the business for themselves. Believe me, they will.

Friendships are gained by learning about and responding to the other person's needs. Marital relationships are built by a two-way trading off of desires to accommodate the interests of another person. And the key to building a successful business is to protect your legitimate interests in profitability while providing the "WIIFM" for your customers.

Listening is hard because it's not passive.

Surprise! Listening is not a spectator sport that can be best accomplished with a remote control from a recliner. I'm convinced that one of the reasons people abandon listening is because they begin with a wrong concept.

First, listening is not a passive activity. Listening is not talking, either. And it's not the useless gap while someone else is talking and we're preparing what we're going to say next. Listening is intensely active. It is hard work.

Think back to a recent conversation. Could it have been anything like this?

Boss: Asks a question.

Employee: Begins to answer.

Boss: Gets the drift of the answer immediately but doesn't believe it is the best way to state the answer. Looks for an opportunity to jump in with a better answer to his own question.

Employee: Keeps talking, just warming up to the subject.

Boss: Realizes he's thinking of his own answer and loses what was being said. Tries to rewind the tape, remembers a few disjointed words. Tries to keep up with the conversation while doing this as it takes a slightly unexpected turn.

Employee: Notices furrowed brow of boss. Assumes high degree of interest in answer. Takes it to a new level.

Boss: Sees a new direction emerging which raises a new question that can really nail this person down. Thinks about how to phrase that question. Needs to remember how the person said it so it can be rephrased in the next question.

Employee: Notices boss looking for a re-entry opportunity, begins to wrap up answer.

Boss: Recapsulizes complete answer and clarifies relationship to next question by saying, "Now let me see if I understand what you are saying..."

And that's just a start. The dynamics of a business conversation like this are much more complicated, but both speaker and listener are usually involved in a great deal of mental gymnastics. True listening involves keeping the mind focused on the task at hand, fighting the natural tendency to take over the talking part, and all the while planning the next stage of the conversation. It's hard work.

Listening is hard because our brains crave action.

Our brains can absorb much more data than a person speaking can deliver. If we don't get enough, we invariably start looking around to see what else we can pick up to fill the gaps. That is why nonverbal communication is so important.

Our brains keep busy processing not only what the person is saying, but all the nuances that go along with it — how the words are spoken, the tiredness in the voice, the little hints at irritation, the few unshaven whiskers that show how the speaker was hurried in the morning. That's also why audio-visual aids are so effective.

Talking while showing an overhead, or illustrating with broad gestures, provide additional information to process. And this is the important part: Listeners will link any additional information to the spoken message, making it more memorable. If there's nothing memorable to link, the mind will usually go searching for something else, and who knows what it will find? Probably a stray conversation in the next cubicle, or a particularly bothersome brand of perfume. Listening involves both hearing and linking the right kind of information.

Interactive media work the same way, because passive listening is so difficult. Our brains much prefer to be engaged in the process, doing something, becoming a participant. Here are a few examples.

Years ago someone tested the idea that people pay more attention when their brains have to work harder. A researcher set up two groups and showed each of them several television commercials. In the first group, the commercials were of the standard variety, with the audio message and video images fitting together as they should.

In the second group, however, the audio and visual elements were totally unrelated. Audio from one commercial was played with video from another. They didn't make any sense.

Recall from the second group was remarkably higher than in the first group. The audience, expecting some sort of logical presentation, had to struggle to find the connections and the logic behind the different messages they viewed. Their brains were engaged in this futile struggle. The result: They paid more attention and remembered more clearly what they were seeing.

Every once in a while a television advertiser plays on the same concept. In one commercial for a Swedish car maker, a man and a woman are driving through beautiful mountain scenery while the man is reciting an odd stream of nonsense. It sounds like an engaging, avant-garde poem or fragments of a crazy dream. But like the two-audience experiment, viewers ultimately cannot figure out what is being said. And when the woman driver smiles at her friend, the name of the car flashes on the screen. By then you're paying full attention. Your brain is engaged. You remember.

Here's another example. When I was a young teen I worked as an evening disk jockey for my father's new and struggling FM radio station. The format was "Beautiful Music" with a lot of orchestral music such as Montovani's 1001 Strings and Andre Kostelanetz. Then a new orchestra leader came out with what I thought was an unusual name: John Andrews Tartaglia.

I remember reading the jacket cover of this new album where it said Mr. Tartaglia had been advised to change his name to John Andrews because Tartaglia was just too difficult to remember. The funny thing is, even though Tartaglia has hardly become a household word, thirty-five years later I still have no trouble remembering the name. I'm convinced the reason is because I had to work at learning to say it. I had to engage my brain in the process. If he were just plain John Andrews, I'm sure I would have lost the memory long ago.

Listening is hard because it takes precious time.

Time is the great enemy of listening, though it hasn't always been so. Sermons were once two hours long, and people sat still long enough to listen. The great orators of the eighteenth and nineteenth centuries spoke and wrote in long, convoluted and elegant sentences. Going to lectures was popular entertainment.

No longer. Today, as a member of the advertising profession, I have often preached the necessity of writing in "bullet" form. These quick little non-sentences provide:

- Summaries of messages.
- Quick, readable information.
- Very little meaningful detail.

As it turns out, however, we not only write in bullet form, we also have come to speak in bullet form. Television and video content is organized around the same principles with information neatly packaged into six-minute segments between commercial breaks. As programmers know all too well, audiences have little patience for anything larger than bite-sized chunks. They need to know where they're at in the program and they need to know when it's going to end.

We expect that kind of structure, but all is not lost. Short attention spans can be inventively engaged to extend our horizons. Ken Burns in his masterful documentaries on the Civil War and baseball used the black title screen as a basic structural tool that not only told people what was coming next, but broke the presentation into palatable pieces that allowed people to stay tuned for hours at a time.

USA Today took newspapers in the same direction, even though it was roundly criticized at first by language and journalistic purists for dragging journalistic integrity into the gutter and making the print media as superficial as television. Superficial? Hardly. The creator of that ground-breaking news vehicle, Allen H. Neuharth, understood fully the lack of patience we have in this Information Age. He made printed news quicker to read, accessible, and exceptionally easy to understand. And by doing so, he further contributed to our impatience.

Most leaders are particularly impatient. While other people in an organization may like to talk details, leaders want to cut straight to the summary. They bulletize for their detail-oriented co-workers, get to the point, and then spend the rest of the time waiting for everyone else to catch up.

Such an approach doesn't always carry over successfully from business to pleasure. Good thing, too. Lovers and good friends passing the time in conversation don't need bullet information. They are quite happy to linger on the details, simply because the point of the time being spent is to spend the time. Listening and talking are done for the sheer enjoyment of the process.

Happily, there is middle ground. If you are successful in building both relationships and business success, you have probably already discovered the magic of listening. You know that the principles of personal relationships have a place in the business setting. You know that you cannot have a great relationship with your spouse, your friends or your co-workers without real listening.

But if this is new, then it's time to work on how you can improve your listening skills — for both yourself and for those who work with you. If you are the listener in a business setting, fight any natural tendency to watch the clock. And if you're the speaker, understand the situation before you say anything. Learn what the listener wants from you, then adapt your style and level of detail according to the listener's needs. Listen, and you'll make friends.

"Fortune knocks at every man's door once in a life, but in a good many cases the man is in a neighboring saloon and does not hear her."
— Mark Twain

3

Two Ways to Improve Your Listening

Think of all the ways you can get the people in your company to do a better job of listening. But first, measure your own skill by running through some of the exercises in this chapter.

And remember, experience talks. Because when you're giving direction to others, it helps if you've run into the obstacles yourself — or at least if you've already established some basic disciplines.

Chapter summary:

- Section 1: Improving your own listening.
  - The 80/20 rule applies to more than just interviews.
  - Land new accounts by listening.
  - Plan what you want to learn.
  - Take notes. It goes both ways.
  - It's not really listening until you loop the loop.
  - Take control with questions.
  - Good listening is wasted without response.
- Section 2: Improving your company's listening.
  - Improve your company's hearing by rewarding listeners.
  - Improve your company's hearing with grassroots polling.
  - Improve your company's hearing with a focus group.
  - Improve your company's hearing with customer check-ups.
  - Improve your company's hearing through formal surveys.

Section 1: Improving your own listening.

There's no doubt that listening can be learned, but listening is a whole lot more than techniques. It really comes down to who you are as a person. Are you sincerely interested in what other people have to say? Do you think others have expertise or experience that could benefit you? Does another person's life and interests hold any interest for you?

You have to answer these questions for yourself before you can become a listener. And though listening skills can be improved with work, ultimately good listening comes from genuine interest.

Unfortunately, that means some people will never be very good listeners because their lives are extremely limited by their own narrow interests. And there's a word for people who are only interested in themselves: *boring*.

Another word may be *lonely*. Or sometimes, in the midst of personal crisis, a person can become totally (and understandably) self-absorbed. They may listen intently to others but only when their friends are addressing their concerns.

This may work for a little while. But no matter how intense the situation, the time will come to get on with life and start showing an interest in other people.

All of us may face such a situation, if we're honest. So if you ever find your self-absorption too high for your liking, the simple solution is to get involved with someone else besides yourself. A good starting point may be a spouse or a close friend, preferably people who need help or attention. But take the time and make the effort to eagerly seek out what is on their minds and what is absorbing them.

The 80/20 rule applies to more than just interviews.

We first applied the 80/20 rule in the last chapter to a first meeting with a prospective client. We've already learned how important it is to listen 80 percent and talk 20 percent.

The 80/20 rule will pay big dividends in other situations, as well, especially situations where you want to:

- Persuade a co-worker you're right.
- Apply for a new job or promotion.
- Reprimand an employee.

- Fix a sticky customer problem.

- Gain support from a colleague.

- Build a team.

- Figure out why your spouse is mad at you.

- Deal with teenagers.

- Get to know a new friend.

Since this book is about business, let's focus on how the 80/20 rule applies on the job — especially how it applies to getting new business.

Land new accounts by listening.

Imagine you're in an introductory business meeting, a meeting where your prospect doesn't know you or your company. You need the business and you are very excited about the opportunity to make a presentation to, well, let's call him Mr. Future.

Mr. Future is a very busy man, well-respected, known to be somewhat tough and aloof. After several letters and phone calls, you are pleased that you secured a 15-minute appointment through his assistant.

As the meeting approaches you're feeling butterflies and thinking about all the things you want to cover in the meeting. But when you realize all the possibilities of issues, concerns, products, services and competition you start wondering how in the world you can possibly prepare to make a really good presentation.

How can you answer his concerns without knowing what his concerns really are?

As you continue to worry, it becomes clear that even if you hauled all your samples, testimonials and sales tools to the meeting, you would probably still miss the boat. When it comes right down to it, you don't have a clue where the boat is.

You don't even know why Mr. Future agreed to this meeting. So you make a list of everything you know about him, things that we have already mentioned. You know that Mr. Future isn't the kind to sit around and waste time. He has a lot to teach you about business development.

You also know (because you read the last chapter) that he will probably prefer to talk rather than listen. So you decide to apply the 80/20 listening rule.

The moment arrives and you find yourself facing Mr. Future in his office. His desk has neat piles of paper but he steps around to greet you, shakes your hand and invites you to sit with him at a round table next to his desk.

"Mr. Future," you say, "I appreciate you taking the time to see me, and I know you are busy so I will keep my promise to limit this meeting to 15 minutes."

He nods appreciatively, so you continue. "I hope to introduce my company to you a little bit and tell you why we are interested in doing business with you, but if you don't mind, I'd first like to know a little more about you and your business."

His expression gives you the green light, so you continue. "I've done a little homework," you say, "and found that Future Enterprises has become one of the leading companies in this market. What do you consider was the most important thing you did in accomplishing that?"

Who could resist such a question? Not Mr. Future, who has thought long and hard on the subject. The fact that you've done some homework leads him to believe that you are someone who can appreciate his success. So he tells you his story and as he winds down you look for your opportunity. At this point, you don't want awkward pauses to emerge as he may start asking you questions.

"I get the feeling, Mr. Future..."

("Call me Bill," he interrupts.)

"Thank you, Bill. I get the feeling that you are not satisfied with this level of achievement. Where does Future Enterprises go next?"

Good question — not just because it is another favorite topic of his, but because it will give you important information you need for your proposal. In fact, both questions will.

The answer to the first question will tell you what his priorities are in achieving success. If he says, "We beat the pants off the competition by undercutting them in price at every turn," you understand something basic about his orientation to the marketplace.

In response to the second question, if he says he is going to focus on improving market share, or consolidate to improve profits, or expand into new markets, or start to retire, he is giving you clues as to his goals and the results he is seeking. But after a few more such questions, you look at your watch.

"This is very interesting, Mr. Future," you tell him. "Unfortunately my 15 minutes are almost up. If you don't mind I'd like to tell you just a little about my company."

Up to this point it's quite possible he has been enjoying himself immensely in the company of what he considers to be a very bright and interesting person, someone who demonstrates unusual wisdom by listening closely to everything he says. So he may say, "No hurry, I don't have another appointment until lunch." That gives you more time for questions, though at some point you need to draw the meeting to a close.

So let's go back to your telling a little about your company. The best way is to link it directly to what is important to him and what he says he wants.

"Mr. Future, you told me earlier that your success was built on commitment to quality, and that you believe your future success depends on improving this level of quality to deal with new price-oriented competition. I'm glad to hear you say that, because not only does it match my company's philosophy, but I think we can help you accomplish your goals of improving product quality. Our products/services can help you become even more competitive in this market-place and this is how..."

This presentation needs to be very brief because its point is only to get you to the next stage — gaining permission to make a formal proposal or presentation.

"Mr. Future, I would appreciate the opportunity to think a little about all the things you have told me here about your company, review my notes and prepare a proposal for you that would show how we could help you achieve your goals. Would it be possible to meet with you a week from today to go over that proposal?"

There's a very good chance you'll get that opportunity. If Mr. Future has absolutely no need for your products or services, fine; he was never a prospect to begin with. But you still impressed him and he may have need in the future or may refer you to someone with need.

If he does have need, you will have impressed him with your intelligence, your grasp of his industry and your place in it. You will also have shown that what is important to him is important to you. You have the beginnings of a positive working relationship.

What's more, you may even have the beginnings of a friendship, all because you decided to actively listen instead of just tell him how great you are.

Plan what you want to learn.

Set goals before you even begin a business conversation. This simple little rule applies to a formal listening situation such as the meeting with Mr. Future, but it also applies to countless daily encounters. It only takes a little thought and a little planning, but the results can be surprising.

Planning provides focus and purpose to almost any business situation, helps you gain valuable information, provides discipline to your listening technique, and builds your reputation as a good listener.

To put planning to work for you, simply ask yourself one simple question before going into a conversation: What do I want to learn?

Here are a few examples you can adapt to your own work situations:

- Interviewing a prospective new employee. *What is this person's ideal employment? How close does this position come to meeting those expectations?*

- Dealing with a disgruntled customer when I am or my company is at fault. *What would it take to recover this person's trust and good will?*

- Presenting to Mr. Future, the prospective new client. *What is really important to him? Does he see the possibility of my contributing to his goals?*

- Talking with my children. *How do they see the world? How it is possible that I can embarrass them so easily?*

- Small talking with friends. *How do they view their work? Which of their values contributed the most to their achievements?*

- Heading for a meeting with co-workers. *Why does John believe that focusing on the details to such a painful extent helps move the company forward?*

No matter how casual the conversation, take it as an opportunity to learn. Do you know what is important to the people you're talking to? Do you understand the situations in their lives that may be affecting their thinking or behavior? Do you know how they really feel about you, your business, your products or services? If not, than ask! When you do, your listening skills will improve tremendously and you will suddenly discover more good information than you ever thought possible.

Take notes. It goes both ways.

As I was discussing the idea for this book with a new friend, she dug out a piece of scratch paper and a pencil from her purse and started taking notes. How could I not be flattered? She thought what I said was important enough to write down, not merely trusting it to memory. That really meant something.

When you take notes, the speaker suddenly becomes more aware of the importance of what he or she is saying. You might even notice a little change in style, as if someone turned a microphone on. Chances are such people will remember the conversation even more because their words, in their mind, have been memorialized on your scratch paper.

Conversely, it can be extremely frustrating when you are providing important details for others, subordinates perhaps, and they are not taking down a single thing you are saying. You know you will have to answer their questions again just because they didn't have the respect for your time and words that note-taking would demonstrate.

Taking notes helps the one who is taking notes, by the way. For one thing, a note-taker is a historian. The person taking notes in a group meeting is the one whose interpretation of the things being said will stand. Remember, historians don't just record history; in many cases they write history, because a record of the past involves selective interpretation.

Note-taking is also a good organizational tool, and at times I have exercised the power of note-taking to gain control of an otherwise unruly situation. I can remember times being in a group meeting with a variety of people, all trying to communicate their strong opinions. The conversation wandered without any clear direction or discipline. My response was to get in front of a white board with an erasable marker, where I could sketch out in a simple form the issues, any areas of disagreement and even the ultimate goal.

Aside from helping bring some clarity, it is amazing what the act of getting up from a meeting and making notes on the board does. It focuses attention and tends to put the note-taker in charge. It makes you look good and it helps you perform better.

The other benefit of note-taking is that you really do learn what you need to know. Your competence and effectiveness in a fast-paced business world demand the ability to take in, store, process, file and retrieve a huge amount of information. That's ultimately much more important than image. If you don't develop a good system, you will be limited by what you can remember.

One caution about note-taking: It can become a distraction rather than a positive part of the conversation. Not long ago I was trying to take notes in a meeting, and the client was talking very fast. I was struggling to keep up, remember what was said, keep track of my ideas in response and prepare the next intelligent question. I scratched out a few notes, but I didn't want her to feel as if she needed to slow down or stop for me to catch up. The note-taking, while certainly obvious, had to be discreet and not a distraction. It can be a fine art.

It's not really listening until you loop the loop.

One of the oldest lessons in listening is the tried-and-true practice of feedback, and I don't mean the high pitched squeal that comes from sound systems. Feedback is simply confirming what the other person is saying by restating it, usually using different words.

Let's go back to our conversation with Mr. Future as an example. You have been asking your prospective new client a number of questions about his business. This is the information you need to prepare your proposal which will say, "Here's where you are going, Mr. Future, and here's how I am going to help you get there."

Suppose, however, you didn't do a very good job of listening. Suppose you thought you heard Mr. Future say he was entering an aggressive growth stage when what he really said was that he was tired and looking forward to slowing down. If you proceed with your proposal based on false assumptions, you'll end up way off the mark and look doubly bad. Believe me, it happens.

One time when I was looking for a copy machine, I communicated my needs as clearly as I could to a salesperson. He made a very good show of listening, nodding at all the right times and smiling in a way that made me think he understood.

So I was shocked when he came back with a canned proposal that completely ignored all my needs. He hadn't listened at all, and only demonstrated disrespect for my time. He could have avoided trouble and made a sale if he had checked his assumptions with a little old-fashioned feedback, using phrases like:

"As I understand you, Mr. Future, you are saying that...."

"Let me make sure I have this correct..."

"I know you explained how you felt about this before, but I'd like to make sure I understand it right..."

"Am I right in assuming that you feel..."

These are all ways to complete the loop. Get into the habit of using tools like these and you will be amazed to learn what you might have missed the first time.

In fact, feedback is absolutely necessary. Without it you can expect that between 30 and 50 percent of everything you thought you heard in a conversation will be untrue. Those aren't good odds when a major new contract or client relationship is at stake.

Be absolutely clear on the feedback issue, since understanding your customers' goals is at the heart of relationship building and satisfying them as clients. In fact, an important discipline to adopt is stating those goals as the first item on any proposal you make. Think of the impact on Mr. Future if your proposal reads something like this:

Future Enterprises

Corporate Goals:

- Growth of 8 percent per year in three major markets.

- Three new product introductions this year.

- Solidify sales organization.

Personal Goals:

- Increase opportunity to spend time away from the office.

- Build leadership and responsibility in key managers.

- Transition key account responsibility to sales team.

If you understand these goals and your proposal addresses these goals directly and specifically, you should be well on your way to making the sale.

But if you miss on your assumptions, everything else is going to be off base and you won't be looking too good. Feedback is the only certain way to keep from embarrassing yourself. Before you leave that conversation, you need to confirm that you have actually heard what you believe you heard.

Take control with questions.

Have you ever watched two people trying to dominate a conversation at the same time? It's a funny sight, as both of them usually try to talk more, louder, or faster. Asking questions is the last thing they would think of trying, but it's the best way to lead.

At first, we might think that asking questions puts all the power in the other person's hand. After all, they are now given the floor. They are the one to be listened to. But it is a delusion. The questioner frequently is the one in control. Imagine yourself interviewing a bright young man for an important position, and he starts asking questions:

"How much do you value someone who is a self-starter, someone who is really motivated and disciplined?"

"Do the people who succeed here have any traits in common? For example, are they normally independent and highly responsible?"

"Can you tell me what hiring the right person in this position might mean for your company and its future?"

Chances are after hearing a few questions along that line you will be convinced you have an eager, intelligent, motivated young executive with the potential to take the company into its rightful future.

Or let's say you are dealing with a difficult customer situation. Imagine the kind of response you'd get to this kind of approach:

"Mr. Madasheck, I don't want to waste your time trying to explain how this situation happened or even who might be to blame for it. I want to get a better idea how this has affected you and your business."

"OK, now I understand the impact of this problem and why it is so serious. What is the best way we can work to prevent this in the future?"

"What do you think would be fair to you in settling this and getting it behind us?"

History proves that asking questions is one of the most powerful communication tools you can use. Socrates used it as his primary means of teaching his students. Jesus turned his critics on their ears by rebuffing their criticism with simple questions they couldn't answer. Good sales staff have always used questions to lead their prospects where they want them to go. Even politicians have start-ed to ask questions.

Now, instead of being sent long, boring newsletters about our local representa-tive's views on the issues, we receive instead a mail survey asking for our opin-ion without too much of a hint about what the politician thinks. It's amazing what a good question can accomplish.

Good listening is wasted without response.

After all this talk about questions, it's good to put things into perspective. After all, good listening is really nothing on its own, even though it can demonstrate care and friendship. If listening does not go beyond listening, it may also demonstrate apathy. Listening is not the end. Good listening is just the means.

Imagine your friend explained to you that his car had broken down and he had an important job interview the next day. The interview was near your office, so he asked if you could pick him up and take him with you to work.

You listen with patience and empathy, giving him excellent feedback so every-one understands.

"I hear you saying that you need a ride tomorrow," you tell him, "and that the only way you can get there is if I give you a ride."

You friend nods expectantly as you think of your response.

"Nah," you finally reply. "I can't help you. It's a little out of my way."

With a response like that, your former friend wouldn't much appreciate your lis-tening skills, no matter how excellent they appeared at first. Don't forget that your relationships will be measured by the quality of your response, not the lis-tening, even though the listening was necessary to create that response.

Section 2: Improving your company's listening.

In the first section of this chapter we focused on ways to improve personal lis-tening. Of course, listening begins there. Now let's broaden the focus to discov-er ways your entire company can improve listening skills.

There is a funny thing about corporate values, though; they invariably reflect the values of the driving force. If you are a corporate leader, that means you.

So if cost consciousness is important to you, the company will reflect that. If superior customer service is important, chances are your company will excel in that, too. And if it becomes clear to everyone that you place a high value on listening to your customers, you can watch for the signs of improved listening throughout the organization. This is just a natural pattern of good leadership.

With that in mind, choose carefully what corporate values you want to take root in your company. It's a lot like parenting. More often than not, your children will pick up the values you live by, whether you intend it that way or not.

I certainly don't want to imply that your co-workers are children. But there's no denying workplace dynamics. If you do not want to leave corporate values to chance, here are a few ways you can improve your company's listening habits.

Improve your company's hearing by rewarding listeners.

Let's say you just spoke with one of your regional sales managers, who relays to you some concerns from a good customer about your number one product. New features offered by a major competitor may cause problems for you, he says.

If you were defensive you might react by saying, "You sales people are always looking for an excuse for not selling what we have. You always want us to redesign our product line just because some competitor throws a new curve at you!"

But you've read this book, and you try a different approach. "Did you find out from our customer what about the competitor's product he liked the most?" you ask.

Once you thoroughly understand the valuable information your sales person discovered, you thank him and tell him he did a great job of listening. Then, at the next sales meeting, you point out what your sales manager found out by listening. You tell everyone this is the kind of valuable information we need to stay ahead of the game, and that you have taken the questions to the product design team for consideration.

As a result, every sales person will come to understand the benefits of listening. They'll be motivated to hone their own listening skills. And the next week, they'll be the ones to bring you some tidbit of market intelligence that may help improve your competitive position.

Improve your company's hearing with grassroots polling.

A new client once asked me to help decide what radio station to use for the retailer's advertising.

"What station do your customers listen to?" I asked.

"How would I know?" was the predictable response.

"Why don't we find out?" I suggested.

"I can't afford expensive research."

"Can you afford to advertise on the wrong station?"

He got the point after I pointed out he didn't need expensive research. He had plenty of market researchers ready to go to work, standing in his store's check-stands talking to the people who had the answers.

We made a simple little form listing the city's radio stations, and clerks simply marked which stations their shoppers listened to. In two weeks we had a clear answer and a media buy was made based on intelligence, not guesswork.

A restaurant owner was in a similar situation, anxious to advertise and increase his business.

"Who are you going to advertise to?" I asked.

"Customers. People who should come to my restaurant."

"Well, then, who are your customers?" I asked. "What are their ages? Are they male? Female? Where do they live?"

"I don't know," he admitted. "I'm not there very much. My son runs the place."

I suggested that waiters and waitresses could keep a simple record of demographic information, even review checks to see where customers lived.

But the restaurateur turned down the suggestion. It would be too much work, he thought. It would be easier and less trouble to buy advertising off the shelf from the sales people who came in the door. The research was never done.

Improve your company's hearing with a focus group.

Marketing professionals love the word "focus group." They've made it seem exotic, difficult, mysterious and expensive. Let's change that.

A focus group is where you focus your attention on the customer or the prospect and learn what they have to say. That's really all there is to it. Yes, you can do that over lunch or in a coffee shop. You can even do it on the phone, although it is much better face to face.

Focus groups, as used in a proposal you would get from a market research firm, would be an organized program to gain insights and information from a group representing your customers or prospects. However, sometimes I get a kick out of the steps some of these professionals take to ensure that the group is "scientifically" selected. With a small sample size, of course there can be no legitimate claim to statistical accuracy.

If you do get involved in a focus group, don't put all your trust in "unbiased random selection" or even in what individual focus group participants tell you. Listen, of course. Listen carefully to what people say about you, your company or your offerings. But remember, the point is to discover trends.

You'll probably find that having a focus group can be an advantage or a disadvantage. Group dynamics are tremendously important and can steer the results considerably. For example, a strong leader in a group can exert tremendous influence over the rest of the group, as can a person with a real attitude problem. You could end up with a rabid fan who distorts other people's views by offering you unending praise, or a misinformed critic who sours everyone's perspective.

At the same time, people in a group tend to draw each other out, ask each other clarifying questions, stimulate thinking and make things more fun. I like the balance, and I like focus groups.

However you decide to do focus groups, the best advice is to do them. Nearly every company can benefit from the unique insights gained during a two- or three-hour session aimed at finding out what people think about your company. It may be painful, or it may be predictable. It is almost never useless.

Improve your company's hearing with customer check-ups.

When Edward Koch was mayor of New York City, he used to walk down the sidewalk asking citizens, "How'm I doin'?" There isn't a company in the world that can't benefit from asking that question.

Tom Peters congratulates leaders of giant corporations who take time with actual customers. Sam Walton walked the aisles of his stores, talking to customers. The best CEOs in the country know what it is to stay in touch with the people they serve.

The benefits of keeping in contact with customers are obvious. Why is it so hard, then, to convince CEOs of medium and small companies to take the time to actually talk to customers personally, face to face? This is the kind of market research that any company can afford.

I call them customer checkups. And there are as many different ways to do them as there are customers. You can:

- Send a return post card questionnaire out with statements.

- Assign everyone (yes, everyone) in the company to call three customers in the next week and ask what's best and worst about your products or services.

- Hire a bright young college student to call customers and ask their advice on how to improve your service.

- Ask salespeople from another company serving your industry what they understand your real reputation is.

- Observe a customer transaction, such as in the checkstand or in a sales presentation. In full view of your employees, ask the customer if they were president of this company what they would do differently. (Note: This takes guts and will be remembered and repeated by your employees.)

- Hire a professional researcher to do a regular, brief and inexpensive tracking survey of customer perceptions.

If you go to the trouble of doing a customer checkup, be prepared for honest answers. Don't go into shock, depression or denial. Do prioritize what you learn and put a simple action plan in place to address the concerns you identify.

There's one more fringe benefit of customer checkups. The process itself will teach your employees how to listen better. Be as transparent as you can in this process, and you will go a long way toward fostering a corporate attitude of listening.

Improve your company's hearing through formal surveys.

To a certain extent, hiring a professional pollster is the easy way out, not necessarily the cheap way out. I am not going to spend a lot of time on it because I believe companies should use extensive formal surveys only when they have internal structured listening at work.

In other words, don't ignore the help and advice a professional marketing and research organization can give you. I can say that with confidence partly because

I'm the president of a marketing and research company and that's how I make my living.

But extensive formal surveys aren't completely effective unless a company is prepared to act on the results. And I am convinced a company is not prepared to act until its employees have begun to work at listening on every level. Before we march ahead with high-powered tools like formal surveys, there is much to accomplish by rewarding in-house listeners, polling at the grassroots level, setting up focus groups and keeping contact with customers every day.

4

What Does Friendship Have to do with Anything?

We have not yet talked about the real value of friendship in business. Relationships, maybe. But friendships? How can you value friendships in terms of dollars and cents?

Certainly the best and most real friendships cannot be bought. But the fact that your business depends on the quality and nature of your relationships with key customers certainly means something. The fact that people who influence others admire or respect you means something else. Now let's discover the real value of these relationships.

Chapter summary:

- A kinder, gentler self-centeredness.
- Being a friend will cost you.
- What makes a friendship?
- The four elements of business relationships.
  - Element one: Awareness — Make sure they know who you are.
  - Element two: Credibility — Make sure they can believe you.
  - Element three: Trust — Make them want to come back.
  - Element four: Chemistry — More than "love at first sight."

Friendship is little appreciated in our day. That's as true now as it was in 1960, when well-known thinker and author C.S. Lewis pointed out that in the distant past, "friendship seemed the happiest and most fully human of all loves; the crown of life and the school of virtue."

But the modern world, he said, virtually ignores friendship. Most men will reluctantly admit a need for a few friends outside their wives and families. But, he quickly added, "it is something quite marginal; not a main course in life's banquet; a diversion; something that fills up the chinks of one's time."

Several decades later, the problem once limited only to men has been adopted by women in leadership positions, as well. Maybe it's a "fringe benefit" of workplace equality.

How did this come about? First and foremost, said Lewis, few people value it because few experience it. "Friendship," he said, "is ... the least natural of loves; the least instinctive, organic, biological, gregarious and necessary."

What was true for Lewis has become even more true for leaders today. But just saying that friendship doesn't come naturally doesn't downplay the growing, almost desperate need many people have for real friendships.

Never mind the 1980s, which *Time* magazine defined as the decade of greed. In early 1990, the editors felt a shift in temperament and decided that in the '90s people would pursue leisure and quality of life with the same aggressiveness with which they pursued wealth and the accumulation of the things in the '80s.

If they were right, both pursuits seem to share a common thread of experience. Both pursuits contain a single, simple theme: What's right and good and comfortable for ME.

Despite what *Time* reported, this relentless pursuit of self-interest has been the human condition since before we were painting rhinoceroses on the walls of caves in southern France. But it does seem that people in other ages acted a little more wisely and applied more balance to the equation.

A kinder, gentler self-centeredness.

As an example, take two people who want to live healthy and happy lives. One eats a lot of fresh fruits and vegetables and gets plenty of exercise. The other smokes, drinks too much, eats potato chips three meals a day and sighs when he has to move to change the channel. Both are pursuing ME, but one seems to do it with considerably more knowledge and insight into what is truly valuable than the other.

The comparison is this: Friendships are good for us. They require us to trade our selfish needs for a greater good. They push us to admit there is a world, a viewpoint, a way of thinking that's a little different from our own.

Friendships also force us to learn. They define who we are. And they remind us that we have value, a purpose for taking up space and breathing the air.

Friendships open new doors as well as new possibilities and new futures. They let us go to sleep at night with the satisfaction of truly enjoying someone's company and believing that someone has enjoyed talking, laughing and being with us.

Being a friend will cost you.

But friendships carry a price tag, not the least of which is time. How many things pull at us, demanding a piece of the limited minutes in a day? Instinctively we understand that before anything else, a time investment is required for any friendship to grow.

A second, related cost is commitment, which in our time has become a thing to be avoided at all cost. In any commitment there invariably will come a time when something else interferes and you grit your teeth and wonder, "Why did I ever agree to do this?" Instinctive or learned, our fear of commitments is one of the major reasons why good friendships are rare.

A third cost is compromise. Perhaps some are "fortunate" in finding friends who always agree, who always see things the same way. Thank goodness, it's uncommon. A friendship of any depth means disagreement; it may even mean out and out conflict. But conflict is not the destroyer of friendships. Friendships are ruined through the inability or unwillingness to compromise, to accommodate, to sacrifice sacred principles.

On the other hand, a friendship that survives misunderstanding and disagreement is a stronger relationship because a higher ground has been claimed. The friendship has grown beyond narrow political viewpoints, beyond churlish words, beyond careless insults, beyond thoughtlessness. At some point, the part of us that says "my pride is at stake here," or "these are my rights" must be murdered and buried in order for real, significant friendships to grow and flourish.

The compromise of pride may very well be the hardest part of growing a true friendship. But once accomplished, such a friendship is like gold tested by fire. The soul is made stronger for the next battle.

Of course, there is no requirement that the friendships discussed here should all be a part of your business. Yet where you find your friends probably shows where your heart really is.

So if you find your friends at the gym, chances are you place a high emphasis on exercise. If all your friends are people you attend church with, church probably plays a big part in your life. If your friends are all at the bar, chances are you have a pretty good thirst.

If you're reading this book, however, business and career success are probably pretty high on your list of motivations. Many or most of your friends and acquaintances will come from this world.

Which leads us to a good question: What's the difference, really, between a business acquaintance and a friend?

What makes a friendship?

One of the hardest things about friendship is accurately defining it. Let's say you are talking to an acquaintance and she asks, "You know Roger Radnoza?"

"Sure," you answer, "he's a friend of mine."

You almost said "good friend." And as you think about it, he's not a friend, just a person you met on a few occasions, someone with whom you had a couple of pleasant conversations.

So is he a friend? Run through your list of close acquaintances. Can you decide who are good friends, who are friends, who are people you know, and who are people you're acquainted with? It's not always easy to draw the line.

There are probably some of whom you can say, "Yes, he's a friend." Others would be clearly non-friends, even though you may like and respect them; and others, well, are people you know. But what makes you feel that one is a friend and another is not?

Lewis has a pretty good scale. He suggests the answer to this question is the sharing of something in common, something of significance to both. A treasure. A burden. Usually there's a time of discovery, when one of you says, "What? You too? I thought I was the only one."

Taken one step further, Lewis suggests we can picture lovers "face to face." In contrast, he explained, friends are "side by side; their eyes look ahead."

In other words, lovers concentrate exclusively on each other, while friends share a deep association around something *outside* of themselves. Perhaps there is a common interest in a hobby or a sport, shared political values, maybe even a shared commitment to God. Whatever the connection, there is something outside of themselves. Their eyes look ahead.

If that makes sense so far, take the idea to work. Shallow or deep, it really does not matter; friendships can thrive at any level. But a friendship cannot last long when goals conflict or there simply are no goals to share.

It's a simple little concept. Friendship is based on the alignment of goals. Remember that definition, because the concept is interchangeable from your personal to your business life. The same concept applies at the workplace. *To build a relationship with a key business contact, find a way to align your goals with theirs.*

Above all, let us be very clear on one point: If we manipulate or if we are insincere in our efforts to demonstrate concern and responsiveness to anyone's needs, or if we show that our interest in any newfound "friend" extends only as far as his orders, we are abusing people. We will richly deserve the lack of loyalty, the derision and the criticism we are bound to receive.

That said, let's look at the right way to build business relationships. There are at least four steps, or elements.

The four elements of business relationships.

Let's say you have decided that relationships with key customers could be improved. You're not yet sure if any of the people will ever be your friend, or even if you want them to be. But one thing is certain. You would do a better job of serving them if the relationships were closer than they now are.

So the question comes up: What can I do to improve existing relationships or build new ones? A business relationship is a complex, personal and dynamic entity; it seems to have a life of its own. But by understanding four critical areas — awareness, credibility, trust and chemistry — we can begin to take the right steps.

Element one: Awareness —
Make sure they know who you are.

Step one to building business relationships may seem so simple and obvious it hardly seems worth bringing up. Yet, if the questions are: "Why am I not getting more from current customers?" or "How do I get new customers?" the answer is usually right here in this first step.

Naturally, new customers are clearly ignorant of what you have to offer them. That is no surprise. So it should also be no surprise that unless they are aware of what you have to offer, a good business relationship can never begin.

What may be surprising is how little your existing customers know of what you can do for them. I can remember plenty of times when my wife and I were thrust into social situations where we finally got a chance to talk with a casual acquaintance, someone we thought we had known for many years. And once or twice, when the other person was refreshingly honest, he's looked straight at me and asked, "I should know this after 15 years of saying "hi" at church, but what exactly do you do for a living?"

Business is the same way. People we think we know, well, they don't know us the way they should. So if you want to increase sales, simply do a better job of informing existing customers of your products or services. If you want to increase your value, tell others about your services. And if you want to increase the value of your company — again, tell others. All the more so if you're growing and changing. People may know what you used to do, but I guarantee you that not everybody is going to know all the new services or capabilities you may have added.

Of course, that's much easier said than done, and telling someone to "just tell others" usually overlooks a simple fact: If someone doesn't already know what you do, they may not care.

Don't take it personally. Your customers have their own lives and concerns; you have yours.

Perhaps you are the engineer who has created a product that you've come to love almost like your own children. It's hard to imagine that others don't have the same appreciation for your work as you do yourself. So you try to interest others in a relationship with you, your company, your products and services, by trying to overcome their own focus on the things that concern them.

I promise you it won't work. It's been tried. You will only gain their attention when what you have to offer becomes part of their focus. You will only convince them when your work shows up on their radar scope as something of benefit to them, something that will help them realize their goals.

And the more significant the goal, the higher will be their interest. But if you can't see a link between something they want and what you are offering, you might reasonably ask yourself: What's the point?

Stop right now and ask yourself this question: How much more business could I reasonably get from existing relationships if they better understood my offerings and how they contribute to the achievement of my customer's goals? If your answer is "not much," then your focus on business development clearly needs to be securing new key relationships.

However, if you see that there is much untapped opportunity in existing relationships, your best strategy will very likely be to focus on strengthening existing relationships.

There's much more to learn about how to build awareness, and we'll take up the subject again when we discuss how to choose the right media. Right now, though, let's go on to discuss the other elements of a business relationship.

Element two: Credibility — Make sure they can believe you.

Step two in how to make a business friendship tells us it is not enough that your customers and prospects know what you have to offer. They must believe that you can perform as promised; they must see your competence line up with reality.

Competence comes when clients believe you are capable of doing what you say you can do. Reliability is the belief that you will come through; that if you say something will be done by a certain time for a certain price, that's exactly what will happen. Even if things get in your way.

There isn't much in this book more important than this concept. If the equity of a business is in its relationships, then the quality of those relationships is determined by credibility.

Credibility is like money in the bank. With it, you can build strength, new business and enhanced value. Damaged or lost credibility, on the other hand, is like a big debt. Your only recourse is to work like crazy to dig yourself out.

Remember this: Your credibility is the foundation to present and future success. So foundational, that any threats to that credibility must be attacked with an aggressiveness likened only to your response if someone should threaten your most precious loved ones.

Another example of the importance of credibility comes from the writings of Aristotle, the late Greek philosopher (not the late Greek shipping magnate). He said that when we want to persuade others, there are three kinds of proof: logos, pathos and ethos.

Logos is logic. Logical proof is powerful in the way it takes the listener through a series of steps called syllogisms, which bring us to undeniable agreement with the conclusion.

Pathos, the appeal to emotions, is more powerful than logos because it reaches the heart rather than the head. But Aristotle clearly considered ethos, "ethical proof," as the most powerful persuasive weapon.

Ethos appeals to the credibility of the speaker, so if the speaker is perceived to be good, wise and right, so will the message. Rhetoricians of all ages have used ethical proof by using the statements of wise and respected authorities to support their statements.

I say, don't believe me but Abraham Lincoln said the same thing and so you should agree with him. Or, Jesus said this, or this DNA expert said this, or the latest basketball star approves of this product. Ethos says you should agree and approve because of the status of the endorsement.

The use of ethical proof is at the heart of good marketing. Remember, we talked earlier about the value of "opinion leaders" in building your business. Building relationships with key people who influence a lot of others is smart and strategic. Building key relations also relies on using ethical proof.

The point here is that you must build and maintain your own ethical proof, which we're calling credibility. Once gained, your personal credibility and your company's credibility provide the basis for a strong future. Once lost, you must work twice as hard to regain it. And if you should fail, you have no future. It really is that simple and straightforward.

Here's some bad news: it's easier to lose credibility than to gain it. Considerably easier.

On the other hand, all it takes to gain credibility is performance over time. You must promise and then deliver. But performing once only gains a little. You need to do it over and over and over just to get to the idea that you are responsible, a performer, that you come through. Do it once and customers may think it is a fluke. Do it year after year and you will have credibility. But fail once, and it may take ten or more successes to balance the impression you leave. It depends on how significantly the customer was let down and what your reaction was to your failure.

Performance depends on both competence and reliability. Competence depends on the ability to perform. And reliability depends on your determination. The customer must perceive that you have both qualities, and the only thing that can convince them is a track record. Your history. What others have experienced. Your reputation. No one is likely to believe bald, bold statements that cannot be supported by a track record.

Here's the catch for young companies. How is it possible to find business without any track record, and how is it possible to build a track record, without first getting business? That sounds just like the dilemma facing young, first-time job-hunters.

Place yourself in their position. As the job-hunter, you have no experience. So you can't sell that. On the other hand, you have your confidence that you can do the job, which is important but not important enough. You're asking an employer to take a risk. And in spite of what many think, business is all about avoiding risk, not taking risks.

So the employers thinks, "I like this kid, he looks like he can do it, but he can't prove it to me. I don't want to have to fire him. I don't want to pay the money that it takes to find out if he'll make it. I don't want the disruption in my business or department that will come from a significant hiring mistake."

The young prospect has only one choice: reduce the risk. He may do it by offering his services at reduced cost or no cost (internship). He may do it by addressing the disruption issue ("Look, if I don't accomplish these objectives in three months, I'll just go quietly away and it won't hurt anyone.") Or he may do it by making the first step easier. ("Why not try me on a single project on a contract? If that works, we'll talk full-time employment.")

The concept applies to young businesses, as well. Instead of asking for the big commitment, ask for a bite-sized one. If you are doing consulting and you're proposing a major contract, suggest phases with commitments on a phased basis. Suggest a small project to start. Perhaps you need a very strong performance guarantee ("I'll be taking all the risk here.").

Regardless of the strategy, you will need to work hard to compensate for the lack of credibility that naturally comes without a track record. And if selling without a track record is scary, try selling when your track record is spotty or just plain bad.

Only a fool who has no concern about tomorrow's business doesn't guard his credibility with his very life.

Element three: Trust — Make them want to come back.

Credibility and trust are closely linked. Credibility is trust that someone will perform. Without a high level of trust no significant business relationship can exist. Awareness and credibility are the minimums for a business relationship.

But what we are calling trust here goes beyond the minimum. It is a bonus, an extra, a luxury. It is the difference between a good customer relationship and a loyal one.

Everyone who is in business wants customer loyalty. If you're in a tough, competitive business you probably spend most of your time figuring out how to get customers who are loyal to your competitors to become loyal to you.

The natural tendency is always to tinker with the price. "I'll buy them," you think. "I'll reduce my price and they'll be mine forever." But the ones who switch because of price are only as loyal as the lowest current price in the market. And you will find, much to your dismay, that many of the best customers stay with your competitor in spite of your great generosity in reducing your margins and cutting your profits. Are they crazy not to switch? No. Just loyal.

Remember, credibility isn't the entire story. A customer may believe you will perform as promised, but they may also believe a dozen others can do the same. There is no loyalty automatically linked to credibility. So if there are ten options to choose from and performance parameters are all roughly equal, then the product or service is seen as a commodity and it becomes price driven. Credibility is not the issue in that scenario.

Here's where trust comes in. Trust goes beyond credibility because it is that thing which creates loyalty. Trust arrives when you believe that someone has your best interests at heart.

Children trust their parents instinctively. They believe in the parental role, that their needs will be met and that they will be protected. It takes a good deal of opposite experience to begin to persuade children that their trust is not justified.

Unfortunately, this kind of trust does not occur as easily with adults. We have banged into the realities of life a little too much. We are like the naturally friendly dog who has become wary and nervous because of ill treatment. We approach new people cautiously, all senses at alert. We cannot always be sure, but we are fairly certain there is a harsh beating behind that artificial smile.

It takes extra effort to get beyond that kind of suspicion. For me to believe you are willing and able to put my interests first, I must believe you have the character to sacrifice your own interests. You have to show me.

Let me give two examples. I had been working with a mid-level manager for some time, my main contact at a very important client. We had done many projects together and had a good working relationship.

One day I learned that someone else in the contact's company wanted this person's job and had begun a calculated attack. This person brought up any failings or weaknesses to my contact's supervisor whenever possible. Unfortunately, the attack was beginning to work and she was talking with me about how she was beginning to feel threatened. The heat was on, and then disaster struck.

A major advertising piece that we had been working on together came back with a significant error. Of course, both of us had proofed it and approved it and even the supervisors had approved it. But given the political climate, my contact was petrified. She made it clear to me in a way I did not understand at the time that it was all my fault.

Clearly the charges were false and uncharacteristic of our working relationship. To make matters worse, things were not going well with my business at the time and I was feeling particularly vulnerable financially. She asked me to pay for the reprinting of this corporate brochure.

It was a cost that would seriously damage the business, one I would have assumed if I had been at fault. But the client had approved the project as is. I prepared to tell her no.

Then I talked over the matter with a small group of friends with whom I was meeting regularly. They understood my business position, but advised me clearly, directly, unequivocally: "Pay it."

"What?" I argued. "I'll have to pay for every mistake they make. I'll be ruined!"

"Pay it," they insisted.

Not understanding them very well, but having utmost regard for their wisdom and experience, I decided they must be right, no matter how I felt. I went to my client contact and said I would pay for the reprint if her boss decided it was a serious enough problem to require that. The relief and gratitude on her face was enormous.

My contact survived her attacker, and her company never ordered any reprints. But I am convinced that the loyalty created there played a significant role in their decision to retain our services when we lost a key employee not long after that.

Here's another example, but this time I was on the receiving end of sacrificial service. My office was destroyed in a devastating flood. A calm, peaceful creek next to my office overflowed its banks one Saturday morning in February and filled my office with muddy water up to the desktop level.

While I and a couple of employees to whom I will be forever grateful spent three hours in waist-deep, freezing water hauling out computer equipment, virtually everything else was destroyed, including my phone system. Numb with the freezing water and disbelief, we hauled everything into a small office space on the floor above.

Since we live in a small town, by afternoon friends and curious onlookers were arriving to check out the damage. One of those who came was the co-owner of the company that supplied my phone system. He saw that my fairly new phone system was underwater and he understood that my financial resources at the time were extremely limited.

Without even asking, this man went to his office, found a used phone system and installed it over the next forty-eight hours in our new little office upstairs. By Monday morning, we were back in business, or at least the phones were working.

I didn't ask him to do that. I didn't have to beg and plead and threaten to get the service. All I knew was that Monday morning I could take calls. That was one of a thousand kindnesses extended to me in a time of crisis, one I will never forget. A customer's problem — even a crisis like mine — is the greatest opportunity to create loyalty.

Now can you imagine my answer to the next phone salesman who came along and suggested that I could pay a little less by buying a new phone system from him?

You know the answer to that question, because loyalty is built when you show that you are willing to serve your customer, even if it means not serving your own immediate interest first. And because that is such a difficult, even startling action, it has impact. The greater the sacrifice and the greater the value to your customer, the more it will mean.

But there is a limit. No customer has the right to ask you to go out of business for his benefit. No customer has the right to ask you to seriously put your enterprise at risk. Customers, even valued customers, don't have the right to go to this well of sacrificial service too often. If they do, they lose value to you as a customer.

In other words, trust needs to be mutual. You are willing to make the sacrifices to meet their needs, as long as you believe they value you and would not ask something of you that would be seriously damaging. Then you must trust that your valued customer also has your best interests at heart. If you don't, their value as a customer diminishes.

Expect it to happen, once in a while. When I was quite young I developed a very unscientific theory that ten percent of all the people in the world are true jerks. I came to this conclusion when I was helping a friend run for public office and was standing at the entrance to a sporting event trying to introduce the candidate. After awhile, we could predict that about one in ten would be rude, crude or nasty. It was quite predictable, really.

Nothing in my life since has caused me to challenge that theory. The reality is, some people are just plain mean, nasty and bad, including customers. And when they are your customers they can absorb a tremendous amount of your time and energy in a futile attempt to make them happy. It even seems that they're happiest when you've made them unhappy. Take away their justification for being angry by being more than fair and you just frustrate them more.

If you find yourself in that kind of situation, it's time to total up your losses and call it quits. But two quick warnings: First, you'd better be darn sure they really do fit in this "jerk" category and you're not just signing them off too quickly because you've failed. If it turns out they're a strategic opinion leader and you didn't do everything you could to make things right, there goes your credibility and reputation.

And second, even if you want to tell them where they can take their complaints, resist all temptation. The way you tell someone you'd rather not do business with them may be just as important as telling a valued customer why you value their business. Help them solve their problems by leading them in a different direction. Show them the door by saying something like: "I'm really sorry the hamburgers we cook here don't meet your satisfaction. Perhaps the ones down the street would be more to your liking."

Remember, a valued business relationship is a loyal business relationship, and that loyalty is frequently created through sacrificial service. The result will be mutual trust. While it's not an essential element of good business, that kind of trust adds a powerful dimension to your relationships and your future success.

Element four: Chemistry — More than "love at first sight."

By "chemistry" I certainly don't mean some sort of biological or chemical attraction as some people describe "love at first sight." Chemistry is something a little magical, mystical and hard to explain when it applies to a business relationship.

And if trust is a bonus to a good relationship, chemistry is frosting on the cake. While it is the least essential of the four elements, the right chemistry makes everything more fun and meaningful.

You know when you "click" with a co-worker, an employee, or even a customer. You know when there is an almost immediate sense of mutual interest and respect. But it doesn't have to happen immediately. Sometimes, the best relationships are built over time. I'm reminded of this when one of my closest friends tells me how much he used to dislike my probing questions and somewhat arrogant, argumentative style. I didn't particularly appreciate the way he used his quick wit and humor to block any attempts to get below the surface of his life. But with time and a lot of discussion we have come to appreciate each other's style.

Chemistry is not something you go out looking for with your business relationships. And there is nothing more irritating than a salesperson who presumes on your relationship by pretending to be a much more intimate friend than you have any desire of becoming. So extreme caution must be applied in making any assumptions about the nature of a business relationship.

That said, you will know when the friendship has gone beyond business. Chemistry, in the sense I am using it, is at work when you realize you would prefer to lose this person's business than his or her friendship. And when that business relationship is one of your most valued, that is saying a lot.

All of which brings us full circle. We began in this chapter talking about the real value of friendships, about how they contribute to the genuine experience of living. We learned that if business is important to you, it is possible that your closest friendships will come from your business contacts. And now it has become clear that those relationships may be even more valuable to you as pure friendships.

That may seem like an annoying complication. But then, this is one book about building business that says building business isn't everything.

"Great minds have purposes, others have wishes."
— Washington Irving

5

The Message

Identifying your company's core message will probably be the most important step you ever take as you build relationships.

No, it's certainly not easy. Identifying your core message requires an objective self-analysis and a thorough understanding of your customers' needs. But you can do it. This chapter will help you define your unique core message and take you through the process of putting that message to work for you.

Chapter summary:

- How important is your company's message?
  - Reason #1 why we need a core message: No one wants a confused customer.
  - Reason #2 why we need a core message: It's a great way to unite your employees.
  - Reason #3 why we need a core message: No one wants to be confused with a competitor.
  - Reason #4 why we need a core message: Having one helps us make the right decisions later.
- Create your message by claiming your word.
  - Step #1 to building a core message: Find out who you are.
  - Step #2 to building a core message: Find out who your friends say you are.
  - Step #3 to building a core message: Let your competition help.
  - Step #4 to building a core message: Create a short list and try some out.
  - Step #5 to building a core message: Translate your idea into a short, powerful statement.

How important is your company's message?

Your company has a message, but what is it? The best way to answer that question is to have you come along with me on one of my casual strolls through Bayview Cemetery.

Reading some of the names, ages and epitaphs is a meaningful experience, even though most of the stone markers give me very few clues. Many include only birth and death dates. A few have messages like "Beloved Mother," or "Then We Shall See Him Face to Face."

Others are military monuments and I know that those people have served in the armed forces; I may even find out their ranks and units and the conflicts they survived or didn't. A few offer tantalizing clues. One, a recent marker that used the new technology of computer-based stone cutting, has a fine image of a fishing boat. I can only imagine how important fishing had been to that man.

Reflecting on these markers has led me to question, though: What would I want to leave behind on a stone monument to tell a passerby all about me? There's much I would want to tell, and so little space. For a moment I thought how daunting it would be to capture a person's life in just a few words.

But if my knowledge of them is slight, then the message is everything. It's all I have to go on. Whether it corresponds accurately to the person is irrelevant because my understanding of that message is everything to me. It is the complete truth, from my viewpoint.

That's why your business message is so important.

And that's why the accuracy of your message is so important, as well. One of the harshest things that can be said about anyone is that they are insincere or putting on a show. How can you know when such a person is speaking from the heart? How can you separate the front they present from the truth? How can you trust them?

Worse yet is if you establish a relationship based on misinformation. Someone tries to fool you about who he really is, maybe for the purpose of winning your favor. When you learn the truth you feel betrayed and abused. Later, if there is any hope for a real relationship, it must start over from a negative position. The person has dug a deep hole and it will take time just to get to level ground.

Businesses do this all the time, perhaps for all the right reasons. They want their customers to like them, to need them, to depend on them. So they bend and twist and change into whatever the last important customer decided they should be. Since that's probably different from what the previous customer had wanted, they frequently put on a different face, a different personality, and send a different message.

The result is a horrible lack of trust. And trust, as we discussed earlier, is one of the building blocks for solid, loyal relationships. It's not something to mess with.

Trust can be built up by identifying — and then sticking to — your core message. But without a core message that can be communicated similarly to all your key relationships and through every level in your organization, you run the very great risk of creating "mixed messages." A mixed message may not seem so dangerous until we understand that it is one form of lying and a major cause of customer confusion and distrust.

Let's first consider why we all need a core message. Then we'll discover how to go about creating and using this message.

Reason #1 why we need a core message:
No one wants a confused customer.

This concept seems so elementary, so common-sensical. Few businesses set out to confuse their customers. But, the reality is that a great many companies do struggle with consistency and suffer the consequences. They do not present themselves clearly, and when they do, the message they send is substantially different from the last one.

A very simple example is the company that does not consider it important to consistently present their logo. This is usually the problem of smaller companies and those who lack marketing experience. But it is surprising how often it is necessary to give a very smart CEO or executive a little lecture on the importance of logo consistency.

The same people wouldn't dream of changing their corporate name on a whim, or think that it wouldn't matter if one day the company was called Johnson O'Reilly Associates and the next day it was called Mechanical Services, Inc. or even O'Reilly Johnson Associates. They can understand how that would confuse the marketplace and threaten their business.

What some fail to understand is that people communicate visually and that a company's logo is visual shorthand. Change the visual appearance beyond certain limited boundaries and the meaning is no longer the same. The result is confusion and a distinct tendency to lose business.

Changing logos is only a superficial example. If you change the way your company is communicated, or if you change the core messages you send, or even if you attempt to change the entire nature of the company, the problem gets very complicated very quickly.

Let's say you started your own landscape service. You had always enjoyed working in your own yard, so you started picking up jobs from friends, acquaintances and family members. That was several years ago and now you have eight employees, you drive a nice pickup with your company name on it, and you are serving a fairly well-to-do and very loyal clientele.

Obviously, you've done a pretty good job of Friendship Marketing. You've emphasized service to the highest degree. If your customers want you to do some extras around their yard, you do it. If they call back wanting the hedges trimmed down just a bit more, you do it. You've built this level of service into your pricing. You're not the lowest price in town and sometimes it bothers you, but your customers expect a high level of service and you have to charge to be able to provide it.

Then a new competitor comes to town, part of a national franchise outfit. They advertise their low prices and start peeling off a few of your lower-end clients. Eventually they even land several of your better customers.

Now you're struggling. You must head off the challenge, but how? You decide you've got to match pricing so you write a letter to your customers with the good news that prices are coming down, but the bad news that some of the extra services you haven't charged for in the past will now be billed. You're surprised to find after this letter that you lose more of your good customers.

The problem is obvious, if you think about it. Your customers became confused when they couldn't find consistency in the way you presented yourself. First you were service-oriented, then price became the issue. They heard mixed messages. In fact, they consider you've been dishonest with them, and now they don't know who you are and what to expect from you. Their trust in you has been damaged. And all this because you were trying to serve them better and stay in business.

Savvy advertisers and marketers do everything they can to avoid creating false expectations. They understand you don't normally have a chance to recover from an initial disappointment. The message that goes out must be true, its offer must be deliverable and it must be consistent.

Reason #2 why we need a core message: It's a great way to unite your employees.

If your business involves employees who deal with your customers in any way (which is just about everyone with employees) you definitely need a core message. It is your main protection against sending out a confusion of signals, and it is a sure way to make sure all your employees are pulling together.

A supermarket catering to an upper income area offered many extra features desired by this market, but the overall prices reflected this. Although no one likes higher prices, most of its customers accepted the trade-off because the store also offered the other things they liked, like deli delivery, fine meats and special organic produce. One day, however, an elderly customer on a fixed income shopped the store and complained to the clerk about what she called exorbitant prices. The clerk not only sympathized but loudly agreed that the prices were far too high and the customer could get much better prices at another store. Unfortunately, the clerk didn't bother to explain the extra features or show how the store excelled in so many ways. Maybe she didn't know how her store excelled because the store's core message had never been explained to her. She had never heard it discussed, debated or endorsed internally.

Take this little test. Go to your employees (not just those who report directly to you) at every level in your organization and ask this simple question: "What is the one thing that distinguishes us from our competition?"

You will know your core message has been effectively adopted if, in their own words, you get essentially the same answer from the people you ask. But without that kind of consistent understanding and "buy in," customers will continue to receive mixed messages about your company and what it stands for. Don't let that kind of situation go unaddressed!

Reason #3 why we need a core message: No one wants to be confused with a competitor.

Not long ago a survey attempted to answer which was more effective in advertising: the use of star athletes, or the use of humor? What would you think?

The answer came back that it didn't matter. Neither was effective if the ad's message did not distinguish the product or service from the competition's. On the other hand, either or both are effective if they are used in a way that clearly sets the product apart. Crystal-clear differentiation is one of the most powerful elements of all effective advertising. (I say one of the most, because I believe there is something even more powerful that we will discuss later.)

I was asked to create an advertising program for a company that was struggling to sell its electronics product in a very crowded business-to-business marketplace. With thirty significant competitors, the leading ten companies all had strong identities and experience in the market. I asked what their objectives were.

"To increase market share," replied my contact, the company's president.

I asked where they stood in relationship to the competition on price.

"About the same, maybe a little higher than most."

"Ah, then there must be some good quality differences, right?"

"Uh, not really. The product does pretty much the same as the other ones."

"Okay," I replied, trying to discover the key, "so have you established any strong customer relationships that you can leverage into new relationships?"

His reply only discouraged me further. "We don't know who our customers are because we sell through distributors and they don't give us that information."

You may recognize this as one situation where advertising was called in to fix a problem that can only be fixed by serious market planning. In other words, a product cannot be effectively promoted in an overcrowded marketplace without very strong and very precise differentiation.

If the customer cannot answer the question, "Why should I buy this product versus the other one?" then you know your product or service is not clearly differentiated. And if your product is not clearly differentiated, don't try to solve the sales problem with advertising, promotion or a bigger sales staff.

Reason #4 why we need a core message: Having one helps us make the right decisions later.

The final reason for developing and maintaining a core message is to help top management or ownership make decisions. And believe me, they need the help! If you're in that position, you know that leadership is generally lonely, sometimes exhilarating, frequently terrifying and almost always confusing. There are so many voices telling you what to do and which way to turn.

If you are smart enough to hire strong, independent people, they usually always have ideas about what to do and where the company should go. Then, of course, you have the customers to pull you in every direction. On the one hand, you think, "They're the customers and that means they're always right and I need to listen to them and respond."

On the other hand, you reason, "If I listen to that customer, then I can't listen to this other one — because he's telling me something completely different."

See the dilemma? In situations like those, your core message becomes a navigation beacon. Ignore it and you hit the rocks. But keep it in focus, let everyone know that you are sticking to your core message, and it will lead you to your destination.

That's easier said than done, especially when free-spirited personalities get in the way. After all, many entrepreneurs are doing what they are doing because they long for independence and freedom. They want nothing more than to throw off whatever constraints they feel are binding them. Business ownership may give them that kind of freedom, but only if they have a young, immature and very small company.

Business owners may also have employees, customers, bankers, shareholders and a whole bunch of other stakeholders who have claims and who by their nature limit the entrepreneur's cherished freedom. But the maturing entrepreneur realizes that he or she needs some constraints, some disciplines, a harness to keep things moving in the right direction. Writer/publisher Joe Bayley once said in a speech I'll never forget that "Discipline is the bed through which the river of creativity flows."

Your message is your river bed. Let creativity overflow its banks and you may enjoy the freedom for a while, until you realize the devastation and disruption you have caused. But channel all those ideas, changes and new directions into that bed and you will find a deep, fast-flowing stream that will take you on a ride that is both exhilarating and safe.

Create your message by claiming your word.

The idea of what I call a "core message" has intrigued marketing professionals for years. Advertising icon Bill Bernbach called it the USP, the Unique Selling

Proposition. And in their book *22 Immutable Laws of Marketing,* Al Ries and Jack Trout call it "word ownership." Their simple idea says that nothing beats owning a word.

Words like "film" and "soup" are currently owned by giant market leaders. Other words like "autos" and "computers" were also once owned by leaders, but the clarity of their position was taken from them by savvy marketers who created new subsets of words. The computer world is an excellent example.

Apple Computer decided to enter the Big Game against Big Blue in 1984. But up to that point, IBM was the undisputed owner of the word "computer." Of course, Apple couldn't even come close to IBM's market resources or marketplace clout, so to attempt a frontal attack and try to grab the word "computer" from them would have been economic suicide. Instead, Apple chose a word that people were hungry for and that IBM wasn't addressing at the time: "User-friendly Computer."

Taking that approach, Apple rode the "user-friendly" label to multi-billion dollar sales, finally losing full ownership of that valued word to Microsoft with the successful introduction of the Windows operating system. At this writing, Microsoft now owns the "computer" word and appears invincible. But the game isn't over yet.

Sooner or later, it's highly likely that an emerging player with a new twist will carve out a seemingly insignificant sideline market and ride it to market dominance. They'll invariably start that process by selecting a niche opportunity that is not properly addressed by the cumbersome industry giants.

The lesson is simple: If you can't own the big word, find a smaller part of that word and stake your claim. This idea isn't just for national giants, either. Do you live in a small town? Who owns the word "insurance?" What about "high quality produce?" The fact that those individuals or businesses own those words in your mind is what gives them their strength in their chosen marketplace.

Take your pick. The core message can be considered word ownership. It can be considered a positioning statement. It can be considered a simple mission or vision statement. It can be an advertising tag line. It can be inscrutably subtle or as direct as a slap in the face. It can be clever and creative or simple and uncomplicated.

Your core message can take a wide variety of forms, but it must conform to three non-negotiables:

1. It must be true.

2. It must offer what your customers want.

3. It must clearly, unmistakably distinguish you from your competitors.

Leave any of these essentials out, and you simply don't have a core message. That's all there is to it. But let's back up for a moment and discover five practical steps to establishing your own core message.

Step #1 to building a core message: Find out who you are.

It's very clear that some companies don't know who they are, or maybe they just don't care about accurately reflecting who they are in their advertising and promotion. That's no way to treat a friend. Friends don't lie to each other, at least if trust and respect are important in the relationship.

You know that messages communicated in the media may be vastly different from messages communicated throughout an organization. A luxury car service manager excused his dealership's poor service in comparison to their excellent advertising by telling me, "Oh, they just said those things to get a lot of people to buy cars. Now that they've sold a lot, they're not saying that anymore." True story!

What's even more obvious are the many ads that communicate a clear message, only to shift messages the next month. You see a message and build expectations about the business, only to find the real experience of doing business with the company very different from your expectations. Negative surprises like that are very hard to overcome.

As a business, you must know who you really are to avoid confusing and alienating your customers. To help you decide this, I've put together two lists of words which you can choose to describe your company. One is a Values list, the other a Styles list.

Try choosing your words with key people in your organization. You may find that the values and styles you assume everyone agrees are critical are not uniformly understood or adopted. Doing this exercise may start some very interesting discussions about who your company really is and why key people in your organization see it differently.

Values:	Styles:
Low Price	Flamboyant
Fast Service	Sophisticated
Highest Quality Product	Down to Earth
Most Convenient	Up-to-Date
Custom Service	Stuffy
Maximum Variety	Thoughtful
Comprehensive Offerings	Aggressive
Most Innovative	Personable

Don't stop here. Add your own words to the list. Use your own system to identify characteristics that best describe your company. If it seems to you that each item describes you equally as well as your competition, that's a good sign you may not know your own company very well. You may want to proceed directly to step #2.

Step #2 to building a core message: Find out who your friends say you are.

Now it's time to go to your customers and ask them to tell you who you really are. Of course, you may believe that you already know who you are, and if your customers think something else, you may believe they're just plain wrong.

You may believe that, but in marketing, as they say, "perception is reality." If there is a difference between your company's self-perception and your customers' perception, they are right and you are wrong. Plain and simple.

If you don't like their perception, you have to change it. Set the record straight, if you like, by correcting misinformation or by communicating a more complete picture. But you must start out with the understanding that in this case, the customer is right.

Actually, you want your customers to tell you two things: who you are and what they want from you. This can get a little tricky. Let's say you have an office janitorial service. You go to your customers and they tell you your key value is "highest quality, most thorough office cleaning." Conversely they tell you that you are definitely not the lowest priced and you are also not the quickest in getting the job done.

When you ask them what they want from you, they'll say they want you to reduce your price and increase your speed. But you will only know what they really want when you give them some either/ors.

So you ask: "Would you want me to reduce my price if that meant I wouldn't move the chairs and vacuum under the desks and tables?" Or, "Would you want me to get the job done faster by being less thorough?"

If the answer is no, you know they value your emphasis on quality. But you probably knew that already, since they are your good customers in spite of their feelings about a higher price.

A supplier once said to me, "I can deliver quality, quick turnaround or low price. Pick two out of the three." Everyone always wants it all, but most people also understand what that fellow was saying. They cannot expect to get everything. In the end it comes down to people making different choices. And that also means you must select the potential customer base, the "right few" who value those qualities and styles that you choose to offer.

Step #3 to building a core message: Let your competition help.

Many otherwise levelheaded business people react strongly whenever competitors are mentioned. Life would be better, they say, if only there were no competition. But sometimes we forget that customers accustomed to the competitive market have a strong distaste for monopolies.

The newspaper in a one newspaper town can't do anything right. If you run the only grocery store in town, your prices are always way too high and your quality never matches those great stores in the next town. We dislike dealing with government bureaucracies in general and the IRS in particular because they have no competition.

But competition is good for us, and not just as consumers. Competition makes us work hard, encourages us to keep improving, and pushes us into niches where we can survive and thrive. You remember what competition did for Apple Computer and Microsoft, how it helped push them to take ownership of a new niche, a growing slice of the competitive pie.

Your competition can help by letting you know which niches are available for you and which are not. Assuming they are bigger and stronger, the wise thing is to not take them on at their strongest point. Remember IBM. And remember

Napoleon, who proved the effectiveness of attacking an oversized opponent at the weakest point. His strategy still works.

Probe for the weaknesses, in this case defined as benefits or values desired by the market but not adequately provided by the competition. As you probe, don't forget that you cannot be all things to all people. Your competitors probably got to be big and strong by understanding this and playing to their strengths. Knowing that fact gives you the opportunity to play to their weaknesses.

This game has been played out with increasing ferocity in the retail arena, especially since about 1980. The giants have come to almost every town and corner. Discounters, mass market retailers, warehouse stores and member clubs set up shop using basically the same formula: volume buying, merciless deal cutting with vendors, deep pockets to absorb local price wars, minimal service, and a continuous barrage of price-oriented advertising.

It's sad to see the reaction of local mom and pop stores, which may often be regional chains including dozens of stores and doing hundreds of millions in sales. But the reactions are predictable. First they come out with advertising that says, in effect: "We're local. Local dollars stay at home. We've been your friends for all these years. Don't abandon us now. Please. Please!"

Meanwhile, the customers are asking: "What's in it for us?" So the local retailers' second reaction tends to be: "Look, our prices are just about as low as anyone else's. Sure, they have bigger stores and more inventory and can buy a whole lot cheaper. But we've cut our prices so you can still shop with us. I know it looks like we've been gouging you all these years, but ..."

The local survivors eventually come down to this kind of message: "Okay, so a lot of people are going to the big discounters. Let them. Because since the discounters arrived we've gotten to know you. You have become our 'right few' friends and we understand you want something more than what you can get in those giant stores. You want _____ (fill in the blank with personal service, quality goods, better in-depth selection of a limited line, home delivery, enjoyable atmosphere, a sense of uniqueness), and that's just what we're providing."

In Chapter 10 we'll discuss a "Price/Quality Grid" to help pinpoint what combination of price and quality your competitors are offering and in the process help you identify where your "right few" want you to be.

In the meantime, the best help your competition can give you is helping you understand you can't be everything to everyone. Then, if you take a good look at what their message is and what values they offer, your message can come quickly into focus. Especially if you are listening to your customer friends.

Step #4 to building a core message:
Create a short list and try some out.

By now you should have an emerging idea of your company's core values, your style, your customers' expectations, and where you stand in relation to your competition. If you don't, keep at it, and realize that you're in good company. Many executives and business owners struggle with the difficult process of translating vague ideas into simple, concise statements.

When a few ideas do begin to emerge, create a potential list and try some of them out. Don't worry yet about the exact wording; that will come later. For now, the important part is capturing the ideas.

Try them on yourself, your key managers and your employees. Most of all, try them on your friends. Your key customers, that is. You'll probably find that what may sound simple is really anything but. So let's look at an example.

The company manufactures "StrongLock," a heavy construction device that splices together two steel reinforcing rods known as rebar. Many competitors have various designs. But this design is radically different because it requires no special tools or special training to install. It is simple, neat, easy, fits into tight spaces and performs beautifully. It also tests stronger than any competitors' product.

But StrongLock faces two problems. Its radical design causes doubts and the product is far more expensive than the competition. As a result, sales are slow. Yet the CEO's market studies show how big this market is, and he is looking for market share. The advertising and sales messages he has produced talk about exceptional strength, easy installation and a broad range of sizes.

Here's where you come in. You're the new marketing manager and your assignment is simple: get sales moving fast. But since you've read this far you know that your starting point is to find a core message for your company and its product. What should that be?

You know you need to focus on quality, not price, and the CEO keeps wanting to talk about independent lab testing of product strength. Fine, so far. But the real answers, you are sure, are to be found with the customers. That's where you turn first.

You talk to contractors who have purchased your product and those who have not. Non-purchasers tell you their reason is simple: too expensive. To make money on a project they have to keep costs down. While the product may be strong, they tell you, the competition's is strong enough. So to them, strength is not an issue. It's simply a matter of price. Pretty discouraging.

Next you talk to customers, to see if their perspective might be different. Yes, it's expensive, they say, but they bought your product on occasion because it is very quick and easy to install. They wouldn't buy it all the time because it costs too much, but they would sometimes, when the time is right.

You pursue this line. When is the time right? When they're behind on a job, they tell you, or in trouble, or a major bonus or penalty is on the line for completing a project on time. Finally it all starts to make sense.

Your customers aren't buying StrongLock as an occasional treat for overworked crews, or because once in a while they don't mind wasting some money. No, they buy it when the costs of taking time are greater than the costs of saving time. With this information, you create a list of core messages to take to your boss:

1. The highest value rebar splice.

2. Strong Lock is the easiest to install.

3. We make everyone else look weak.

4. StrongLock is the splice to choose when time is critical.

5. It's expensive but worth it.

6. The best combination of strength, easy installation and customer service.

We could have a happy ending to this story, or we could make it realistic. The realistic ending is that someone along the decision chain is going to go for #6. It's the safe one. It hits all the key features. It's the most likely to catch the broadest segment. Makes perfect sense, doesn't it?

Maybe, until you realize that option #6 bears no relationship to customer needs as defined by them. The thousands spent on advertising and promotion with that as a core theme will go largely wasted. Don't let it happen!

Sure, after disappointing results you or someone else could say, "Well, at least we got our name out there." That's the consolation prize of ineffective advertising and there is limited benefit to that. But the opportunity to capture attention and interest will be wasted on an attempt to "cover the most ground."

Look at the list again and choose the one that matches what you learned from your customer. Yes, the core message that best reflects what the customers have told you is #4. It says you don't choose the product for every use and every occasion, but when you really need it, nothing else will do.

Armed with that conviction, a little research might then show what percentage of construction projects are under the gun. From that you might determine that a sizable sales volume is possible by getting a high percentage of time critical jobs. It will focus your media selection on communicating with construction companies that may get into tight deadline situations. Companies that deal in emergency response, highway construction, or office buildings.

Most of all, your core message will help you focus your message on the one critical factor that your friends have told you is important in this example: time savings.

Step #5 to building a core message: Translate your idea into a short, powerful statement.

Back in step #4 it was more important to capture your core value and discover the genuine idea behind your company. If you followed directions, you resisted the temptation to dwell on the exact wording.

Now it's time for a little wordsmithing. The best way to do that is to state your ideas as simply as possible, in sixth grade language. (Sixth grade reading skill seems to have become the de facto standard for most of us in communication. Perhaps we took a clue from *Reader's Digest* and decided that's where most adults ended up.)

Sometimes you will get lucky and the simple, straightforward way of describing your core message also makes for a great headline and tag line. More often, you will need a stronger, simpler statement that will bring punch to your internal communication, advertising and promotion.

First, a definition or two. A tag line is simply the logo-ized form of your core message. The kind of tag line you need (if you need one) depends on your name, your awareness level in the marketplace, and whether or not you are satisfied with the current understanding of your company name.

A tag line may serve as a valuable tool to define, strengthen or modify your public image. "Service Identifiers" are simply tag lines that help tell what your business does. So an "interconnect company" sells business telephone systems. These kinds of companies often sport high-tech names like "Intermax" or "Matrix" or "BTS." But to prevent customer confusion they may have to add a service identifier such as "Business Telephone Systems."

Service identifiers differ from tag lines that are used to communicate a core message. In a real example, (my brother and the staff of his business telephone business) decided that simplifying the confusing world of telecommunications was their core message; they came up with "Making it Easy." When added to their logo or advertising, it became a tag line, not a service identifier. In their case, since their company name is Baron Telecommunications, a service identifier is not needed. The tag line works just fine.

In other cases, a service identifier and tag line will work together to accomplish both purposes. If my brother's business name was Connex Systems and his core message was simplification, he might need a service identifier/tag line like: "We Make Business Telecommunications Easy." The problem here is that just saying it isn't very easy.

Here are a few tag lines from my advertising memory banks. You decide what the core messages are behind each one, whether or not they also identify the service, and how effective they are.

Fly the Friendly Skies	Be All That You Can Be
You Deserve a Break Today	Imagine the Possibilities
We Do It All For You	The Colors of Your Life
It's the Real Thing	The Fabric of Your Life
Mmm Good!	Just Do It
The Cheese That Goes Crunch	The Power to Be Your Best
You're In Marlboro Country	The Low Fare Airline
Food, Folks & Fun	We Try Harder
Plop, Plop, Fizz Fizz, Oh What a Relief It Is	

Did you find any core messages? What about our "SuperLock" friends? Let's say you, as the marketing manager, were successful in arguing your way to #4 as the core message ("StrongLock is the splice to choose when time is critical.") Congratulations. Now you can build some business on that idea.

But first you need to translate your core message into a statement that you can use to communicate. It needs to be strong. It needs to be quick. It needs to be on target. Something like the famous advertising lines that I just listed. (They have remained in my mind for years, which has to mean something.) After just a few moments, your creative mind produces a list that goes something like this:

It's Simply a Splice of Time.

It's Simply a Matter of Time.

The Money Saver When Time is Money.

When Time is Money, StrongLock is the Splice.

When Saving Time Means Real Savings.

Now you're just getting warmed up. You're playing with words like "time," "money" and "savings." And here are a few more ideas: "Put on a Lock on Lost Time — a SuperLock." "Who Says You Can't Buy Time?" "SuperLock Can Save the Job — And Your Bacon." "SuperLock: The Job Saver."

You write fast and furiously, letting nothing stand in your way. As a creative type you understand that when you are in this mode there are no "bad" ideas. You set a goal of twenty ideas, maybe thirty ideas, and when you stall you put it away for a little while. Later you're amazed at how fresh ones come when you return to the task.

This is the fun part of marketing, so you find yourself working on your ideas while you're standing in your morning shower or waiting in a rush hour parking lot. Finally you have your list.

What's best? You've lost your perspective. Some of the ideas look like they might make good headlines or paragraph headings in a product brochure. Some are clearly throw aways and you wonder what you were thinking to come up with those. But the tough choices remain.

What tag line goes best with your logo? The words will permanently fix the message in your customer's minds. And which headline is best to carry the multi-thousand dollar ad campaign you are planning?

You think about going to the boss. It's his money, after all. But no, you realize he will probably just tell you why you should go to message #6, the safer route. You're stuck with the decision, all alone, without friends. Friends!

Yes, you *do* have friends. Customers who are buying your product. And you have prospective friends who would buy the product if they only clearly understood how and when it would help them. They'll help you. They'd love to. After all, you're only asking their opinion, and there are few things people are more willing to give than their opinion.

So you ask them. You call them up on the phone. You ask to meet with them for a few minutes. Or you write them a personal note. You fax it, or send it by e-mail. Whatever you do, you ask and then listen.

Of course, marketing is not a democratic process and headlines and tag lines should not be chosen by committee. Ever. But you, as the decision maker, assemble the best input you can, contradictory as it is, and you make the very best judgment you can. Then, knowing that you have worked through a complete and rational process, knowing that marketing is an art, and knowing that you have a good sense for these things, you move forward to the next chapter.

"I hate television. I hate it as much as peanuts.
But I can't stop eating peanuts."
— Orson Welles

6

Making Friends
with the Media

Our business roots go to the merchants and traders plying the dangerous Middle East
trade routes in the time of the pharaohs, and to the shoemakers and coppersmiths
operating from shelves hanging in the windows of their homes in medieval cities.
It was all personal business. They knew their customers and their customers
knew them. Furthermore, they got new customers from the old ones telling
the new ones where to find shoes or pots.

Back then, personal relationships were primary. Of course, they still are today. But
let's take it a step farther. If you could conduct all of your business on a
one-to-one basis, what could possibly be wrong with that?

Chapter summary:

- Look what Mr. Sears created.
- Rule #1 for dealing with the media: Avoid it, if possible.
- Rule #2 for dealing with the media: Don't ask the media to do what a personal contact can do better and for less money.
- Rule #3 for dealing with the media: Choose the media carefully. Very carefully.
- Rule #4 for dealing with the media: Speak the truth, consistently.
- Rule #5 for dealing with the media: Respect the distractions.

If it were possible, conducting all our business on a one-to-one basis might be a lot of fun. But at some point someone put up a sign and someone else tacked up a little handwritten poster to advertise their wares and how to find them.

Gutenberg came along, made a machine to print the Bible, and soon newspapers were created. Publishers found they could add to their revenues by making room for messages from merchants.

Here in the New World, a rapidly growing population in the Wild West longed for the things that couldn't be purchased in the general stores of their frontier towns. Many of the settlers had enjoyed the easy availability of goods in the East. So a couple of enterprising men, Sears and Roebuck, accommodated them by providing a catalog of goods from which they could purchase what they needed without ever having to come in and talk to anyone. The business of doing business through the media was in full swing.

Look what Mr. Sears created.

Today, doing business face-to-face is almost an anomaly. We go into the fast food chains and there are still young people to take care of us, but the proprietor is usually far, far away. We bank by punching buttons on a little keyboard and wait for a machine to feed us cash. We find entertainment sitting at home watching a parade of items flash by us, then reach for our telephones to place our orders.

From the shopping channel to banking by phone, more and more services are done by responding to computer-controlled voice prompts and punching in an endless series of numbers.

As a result, the media have become far more than a means of communicating. The world is a far different place than when Will Rogers quipped that "All I know is what I see in the papers." The media — and I'm speaking here mainly of electronic media — have become a means of doing business and therefore, of living.

The media are probably also the primary cause of confusion and anxiety among people who are assigned marketing responsibility. They will tell you that the media are expensive, intimidating, almost always disappointingly ineffective, and (did I say?) expensive.

In other words, if you are in charge of spending your company's precious resources on the media, you face the task with considerable trepidation. You know that your chances of hitting on the right combination of approach and results are not very good.

So to help you accomplish your media planning with a little more wisdom and confidence, and to help make the choices that will do the most while spending the least, here are my five rules for dealing with the media.

Rule #1 for dealing with the media: Avoid it, if possible.

I understand this advice sounds a little cynical. A little like the doctor telling the patient not to get sick if they can help it.

But the point is a serious one. Far too many business people at all levels and in all sizes of companies buy media time or space first to solve marketing problems. What they find is that rather than fixing their problems, they quickly add a new one: less cash. And usually the problems they started with still exist.

Using the media for advertising or promotion cannot solve fundamental marketing problems. A TV or radio ad cannot fix your customer count if you haven't been listening to the customers you already have. The media can't cure problems caused by faulty pricing strategy, lack of focus or inadequate product differentiation.

The bottom line is this. If you face marketing problems and you use the media, you will find afterwards that now more people know about your marketing problems (assuming you used the media effectively). If you are not certain of the problem you are trying to fix, avoid using the media. It is not a test bed for problem solving.

You might say there are two mistakes a business person can make about the media. First: "Oh, sales are down. We'd better advertise." And second: "Oh, sales are down. We've got to cut our advertising budget."

In those situations we're seeing the media used not just as a way to solve fundamental problems, but also as a temporary fix for sales or cash flow problems. As one of our former presidents might tell you, that's "voodoo (media) economics."

Certainly, we might advertise when sales are down and we may even cut our advertising budget for good reason. But too often the media become our first target when business decision makers simply don't understand the dynamics as they should. They make their decisions on the wrong basis and their disappointment with the results only adds to needless confusion and the mysterious nature of the media.

There is a time and place to use the media in developing your business. The trick is knowing when that time is right, which media to choose, and how to go about using it. Read on.

Rule #2 for dealing with the media: Don't ask the media to do what a personal contact can do better and for less money.

If you turn first to the media to help solve a business problem, you may find out later that the job could have been done better through other more personal means. Not long ago an owner of a small home and office design firm came to me for marketing help during a slow time.

"The construction economy is weakening," he told me, "and I need to pick up some additional business. I've advertised before without much success. Now I've come to you because I need some professional help with advertising."

"Okay," I continued. "Now, of all the buildings you design each year, how many of those come to you as referrals from other people?"

He thought for some time. "Almost all of them."

"Are there any people who have referred many customers to you?" I wanted to know.

It turned out there were two or three key contacts that resulted in a very substantial part of his business. One was a real estate agent who had a strong position in an important upscale development area. The other was an owner of a major housing development.

"You know," I suggested, "if so much of your business comes from so few people, doesn't it make sense to try to add a few more people to your key referral list?"

We discussed some potential high profile real estate professionals with good business among upscale home buyers and the development community.

"Okay," he asked, "Now how do I advertise to them?"

Wrong question. Certainly I could have suggested the local newspaper, a radio station that carries news they might catch. Even some real estate publications they were sure to read. But we already knew the potential contacts' names. We knew where they worked. We knew their phone and fax numbers. I made a radical suggestion.

"Why don't you just call them up and see if you can meet with them, maybe even buy them a cup of coffee?"

This is not an unusual example. Many times we have identified a very small, very important group of key people. We could spend far less time and money reaching those contacts personally than by creating and executing an expensive ad campaign.

Clearly the 100 percent personal approach is not the answer for every marketing situation, perhaps not even for most. But instead of immediately jumping to the media, most businesses should first make use of their employees and their contacts to build valued customer and key contact relationships.

Sooner or later, it becomes obvious that using the media is not only unavoidable, but wise. When you come to that realization, consider the next point.

Rule #3 for dealing with the media: Choose the media carefully. Very carefully.

How do you define "media," other than as an awkward plural for medium?

Most of us would say the media are advertising channels such as television, magazines, newspaper or even direct mail. But that's not entirely how Webster defines it, and his definition is very instructive.

> **me·di·um** (me'di-um), n, [pl. MEDIA] 1. a) something intermediate. b) a middle state or degree. 2. an intervening thing through which a force acts.

An intermediary, an intervening thing. That kind of definition suggests something in the way, something that stands between where we are now and where we want to be. Sort of like a glass wall that separates lovers, it keeps you from close contact with those people who are so important to you.

If you understand the media in this way, you understand how it becomes more sensible to deal directly with your audience whenever possible. But if you are separated from someone close to you, the intermediary becomes a necessary, if awkward, link. A necessary evil, yet very much appreciated. And again, only if you cannot reach that important person directly.

Suppose you are separated from your loved one by an ocean, and you must communicate. You look for a bridge, a link, an intermediary, a medium, and you have several options. The mail. FAX. Telephone. E-mail. Video conference. Public notice. Newspaper ad. Television broadcast. Choose one, but how?

You could take into account the convenience (especially to your audience), the appropriateness to the message, and comparative costs. Let's create a little decision matrix of these criteria.

Medium	Convenience	Appropriateness to message	Cost
Regular mail	Very, delivered to home	Yes; private, personal handwriting	Very low
FAX	Need FAX machine	Mix; less private, shows urgency	Low
Telephone	Yes, rings in home	Very private, direct voice contact	Moderate
E-mail	Need computer, modem	Mix; private but appears cold	Very low
Video conference	No; set up or find facility	Mix; not personal but direct view	Very high
Newspaper	Yes, pick up at newsstand	Read by everyone	Ridiculously high
Television	Yes, signal to home	Seen by everyone	Yeah, right

Of course no one goes through this kind of disciplined decision process when deciding how to get their message to a loved one. The decision isn't that complicated. Unfortunately, many marketers also don't go through this process when trying to decide what medium to use when communicating with their important people. They should. If they did, they would choose advertising and promotional media using the same criteria:

1. Is the medium convenient to my audience?

2. Is the medium appropriate to the message to be conveyed?

3. Is it cost-effective?

Notice one thing right away. The answer to these questions depends on knowing your target audience exactly. Who is supposed to receive the message?

If you struggle with these questions, we've hit on the main problem most people seem to have about media selection. They don't know to whom they want to talk. For instance, if you want to send a general love letter to potential mates across the ocean, using the newspaper or television might be the most effective tool. Just don't set your expectations too high.

Keep in mind that making the right media choice depends above all on having a crystal clear definition of your target audience. The clearer, the better. Without that, don't even start this process.

Assuming you know who your important people are, find out next which media are convenient to them. Or rather, discover the media that are a part of your target customer's lives. Which magazines do they read the most? Is there a newspaper that has become a part of their daily routine, and if so, which section? Is there a television program they won't miss, or a category of programming? Are they commuters who listen to the radio?

Sometimes you can get the answers you need through media sales representatives. Give them a clear definition of your target customers and have them tell you how close they can come to efficiently delivering your message.

On the other hand, you can ask your target customers yourself. Naturally, I prefer this alternative, although the information you gain from honest, straightforward media representatives is usually extremely valuable. There's just nothing like hearing it directly from your loved ones' mouths.

Once you find out which media are convenient to your beloved customers, we still have two questions to answer: compatibility with your message and cost effectiveness.

Compatibility asks, is this the kind of medium where your customers would expect to find a message from you? Certainly there could be a great advantage to springing a surprise on your loved one; say, a proposal over the loudspeaker at a soccer game. But only the novelty makes this kind of approach work; if you wear it out by using the novel approach for every message, you also wear out your effectiveness. ("Paging Miss Vickers; Mr. Calloway would like to know if you are available for dinner tonight. And the Panthers have just scored another Go-o-o-o-a-a-l!")

Just because your customers might expect your message doesn't mean the medium is right for you. You message and your company must also match something called "editorial environment," which is the quality, character and personality of the information format.

Think of the difference between, say, *Time* magazine and *Spin*, an alternative newsmagazine for people who are more comfortable with an MTV approach to life. If these two magazines should cover the same information, as occasionally happens, you can expect the treatment of their coverage to be quite different.

Another example is the difference between "60 Minutes" and "Hard Copy." Both are television journalism programs in the news magazine format, but the editorial environment differs considerably. And the environment heavily influences the message.

If I see an advertising message in an environment I respect, trust or admire, I may be influenced and more receptive to that message. At the same time, if you find out that your target customers are strongly drawn to a particular editorial environment, that fact speaks volumes about them. Their viewing habits are an important clue for you, helping you to discover what they in turn may expect of the style and personality of your message.

The point is to be aware what the editorial environment of the media can do to the message you place in that environment. Put a clean message in a polluted environment, and you can expect some pollution to spill over into the message.

Then there's the cost-effectiveness question, illustrated by the fellow who invents a new software program and determines that anyone who uses a personal computer is his target audience. Through a couple of industry contacts, this bright inventor figured that the only way to reach his audience would be through one of the glossy national computer publications.

But he was in for a rude shock the first time he priced a small ad. He quickly decided that on his budget he could probably only afford a one-line classified listing, not the quarter-page ad he had envisioned.

Our friend's problem, though, was not the cost of advertising. His problem was that he had not done a very good job of defining his target audience.

The better job you do of identifying the "right few," the more you are driven to media that are more personal and less mass. And here we find a strange phenomenon. The marketing media generally believed to be the most expensive often turn out to be the most cost-effective, and the media viewed to be the least expensive (in the traditional method of measuring called cost per thousand) turn out to be the least cost effective. Here's what I mean, in very rough figures:

Medium	Cost Per Thousand (CPM)	Calculation Basis
Personal sales call	$275,000	(average of $275 per call)
Personalized letter	$1,250	(prepare, print and mail)
Local Radio	$13.30	(rate: $40/spot with audience of 3,000)
Super Bowl	$9.29	(audience of 140 million, $1.3 million for :30 TV spot)

By the traditional measure of cost-effectiveness, you should run right out and book your TV time for the next Super Bowl. And you'd be right if you have concluded that this is the best way to find the "right few."

But if you read the earlier chapters of this book and have concluded that your strategic relationships are found within a small and narrowly defined group, you'll find yourself moving up the cost effectiveness chart to the more "expensive" media. If you can find those five or seven people who will make all the difference to your business, the cost of a personal call becomes quite insignificant.

Rule #4 for dealing with the media: Speak the truth, consistently.

Many marketers mistakenly believe the media have no connection with their everyday work of meeting customer needs. They believe they are starting with a clean slate to create an image that the customer wants. What's worse, the image they believe the customer may want often changes from week to week or month to month. Caught up in the fun and drama of producing a media message, or being on TV, they happily remold their business in the image of the latest customer whim.

If a clothing store owner has effectively positioned her small business as a purveyor of quality clothing, for instance, she must do everything she can within the media she uses to protect that position. If she has selected good lines and emphasized considerate customer service, her customers can rightfully expect to see that emphasis carried through in all her advertising.

So if she suddenly succumbs to the temptation to run a big, bold price-only ad in her local newspaper, the results of such a Jekyll & Hyde message will be disappointing. A classic case of mixed messages, media-style. If she meets the discounters on their media turf, she effectively tells her loyal clientele: "We really didn't mean what we told you before about quality and service. If low prices are important, now you can shop here."

The message from the upscale clothing store is simple. Your company has core values that are understood by your existing customers, core values that make your business what it is. But mess with those values in your advertising and you mess with the very reason your customers are doing business with you. How many times have you seen a blowout sale on a new Mercedes?

In other words, make very sure your advertising messages through the media are completely consistent with the values of your business as understood by your customers. Do not miss this point.

Knowing the danger of slipping on this issue is one of the main reasons to identify what makes your business unique. Write the values down. Commit them to memory. Make sure everyone in your business understands them with their heads and their hearts. It is through these people that your core values will be communicated and protected.

The same holds true for your media messages. If you work with an advertising or marketing firm, or if you do a lot of business with a media representative, make sure they thoroughly understand your core values. Take the time to educate them. And don't be afraid to point out to them when they are off base, if they bring you ideas or messages or styles that are inconsistent with who your company really is. Guard your core message with your life.

Remember the story of Cyrano de Bergerac, the long-nosed fellow with the golden tongue who stood in for a hunky guy who sought the love of a beautiful woman? The hunk wanted her, his "right" one, to believe that he was what she wanted him to be, not what he really was. His words were truthful, but not for him. They were consistent, but not for him.

As the latest film version has it, the beautiful woman went with the ugly competition in the end because the guy with the nose spoke the truth and spoke it consistently. We run the same risk of losing our customers to the competition if we don't keep our media message completely truthful and consistent. Don't forget, Cyrano and the girl lived happily ever after, leaving our jilted hunk to try yet another new advertising gimmick.

Rule #5 for dealing with the media: Respect the distractions.

As a communications consumer, we face a blizzard of messages that would have driven our great grandparents crazy. One estimate has it that every person in the U.S. is the target of 21,000 ad messages every day. And just one company, Proctor and Gamble, spends over $2,000,000,000 (that's two billion dollars) a year trying to get your attention and affect your behavior.

That's just the advertising business. Add the music business, the movie business, the news business and the television business. Some of the best minds in the world are working overtime every day, doing their best to make you pay attention to their messages, right now.

I know this, and you know this, and almost any intelligent marketing person would know this. But somehow when those same marketing people craft messages and throw them out into the media blizzard, they expect the world to come to a grinding halt while everyone stands for a moment of silence and concentrates on their message of price and item.

Of course advertising doesn't work like that in our media-saturated environment. Actually, advertising is a little like spitting in the river. Sometimes I think advertisers, after spitting, want to shout, "Watch out for the flood!"

There is, however, a good side to this media proliferation, because it creates more choices. When I was growing up there were only a few magazines to read, magazines like the *Saturday Evening Post, National Geographic, Time, Life* and *Look.* Today the variety seems endless. Every little industry group has several magazine choices.

Most communities have their own little publications, as well, often covering local business, senior citizens, regional gardening ... you name it. The good news is that you can use this incredible selection of media to get to the "right few" if you think about it creatively and work hard at making the right media choices.

The bad news is that with so many voices, you have to work extra hard to be heard. But we've already seen how carefully selecting media can help the message come through. Generally, the smaller and more targeted the media instrument, the more effectively it will serve as a platform.

And that's not all. Media professionals use two more techniques besides targeting to get their message through all the distraction: creativity and frequency.

Creativity in this sense usually means doing the unexpected. If you are used to seeing pages of gray type in a newspaper and you come across a totally black page, or white page, or red page, you'll probably give it a glance to see what all the fuss is about. At the same time, there is good creativity and bad creativity. Bad creativity attracts attention with techniques that have nothing to do with the differentiating message. And when people discover that they've been had by an attention-getting gimmick, their wrath quickly turns against the advertiser or the product. Believe me, it's never worth it.

Good creativity, on the other hand, has everything to do with the differentiating message. With the right kind of creativity, your message will burst through the clutter and you will communicate your company, product or service in a truthful way. This is the kind of message people will turn the channel to see. This is the kind of advertising message people will pay to wear on their own clothing. If you manage to pull off that kind of creativity, give yourself or your ad agency a raise.

One of the best examples of breakthrough advertising creativity was Apple Computer's 1984 television ad. It sent a stirring message about how the tyranny of Big Brother (Big Blue/IBM) was being broken. It was one of the most memorable ads of all time and demonstrably one of the most effective. What was most amazing about the ad, however, was that it ran only once, during the Super Bowl of 1984. With that kind of creativity, you needn't rely on the third method of breaking through the clutter — frequency.

Children use the frequency method instinctively and to their advantage. If Mom or Dad don't change the diaper immediately, they turn up the frequency and persistence of their cries. Works every time. A little later, if Grandma hesitates about buying that toy in the window, they ask again. And again.

I won't carry the childhood pattern to an extreme. But you're probably not surprised to know that direct mailers insist you must send the same appeal to the same mailing list three times for optimum results. Once is simply not enough. Radio advertising researchers have also demonstrated that the same person must listen to the exact same radio message at least three times before they have even really heard it. (Your kids could have probably told you that.)

You say, no problem. You can run your radio ad three times. The trouble is, to catch those same people three times you may have to run the ad much more than three times. Remember, these people are switching from station to station, moving in and out of their cars, doing a thousand other things and hearing and seeing thousands of other messages all the time you are trying to reach them.

Listen to your kids. Effective use of the media demands frequency. You've got to repeat your message, or waste it.

*"The strength of the Pack is in the Wolf, and
the strength of the Wolf is in the Pack."*
— Rudyard Kipling

7

Creating the Team

*In Chapter 1 we said relationship building is a team effort. If only doing it was as
easy as saying it.*

*"Okay, everyone, we're going to go out now and build a team to create the strong,
loyal relationships that our business will depend on for the next ten years.
Ready? Break!"*

Chapter summary:

- The Horse and Wagon Story.
- Why is the leader in the harness?
- Why are the horses in back?
- Why the horse climbed into the wagon.
- Teamwork is the "Power and the Glory" of Friendship Marketing.
- Creating your team.
  - First, define winning.
  - Next, integrate team winning and individual performances.
- Measurement: A little scoreboard magic.
- Recognition: More important than money.
- Compensation: The way to focus attention
  - Pay communicates what you really expect of your team.
  - Link pay to individual performance and team performance wherever possible.
  - Competitiveness today requires new approaches.

- Match your pay system to your team's personal styles and aspirations.

    1) Identifying roles: Recognize diversity.

    2) Which comes first, frontline or support?

- Dealing with obstacles helps maintain the team.
- Using SALT helps to build the team.
  - Strategic relationships.
  - Alignment of goals.
  - Listening
  - Teamwork

I wouldn't be a bit surprised to find out that here is where most of the readers of this book will find the most difficulty. Creating a cohesive, motivated, focused, dynamic, productive team is the overwhelming need and desire of virtually every business owner or executive with whom I have had the privilege of working. While almost everyone thinks his or her situation is unique, the complaints and comments start to sound like a well-tuned choir:

- Why can't my people think more like business owners?

- How do I get them to take a little more initiative?

- I pay them well, we've got a good bonus plan, so why is productivity still such a big problem?

- Why do they take so little interest in the things that really matter to this business?

- Why can't they think for themselves?

- It seems they just want a job and someone to tell them what to do; why can't they come to me with thoughts and ideas instead of expecting me to do it all?

If these questions sound familiar, or if you can relate to the frustration and the sense of helplessness they reveal, you've come to the right place. After a few years of hearing the same sort of puzzlement, I came up with a little analogy that seems to strike a chord in many owners and executives. I call it the horse and wagon analogy, and I'll trot it out one more time.

The Horse and Wagon Story.

Business is like a wagon. You, the owner, feel like you are in the harness pulling the wagon with all your strength. You look behind you and you see all these workhorses that you recruited, trained, paid for and motivated. They're all sitting in the back of the wagon enjoying the ride. They're not entirely happy about the situation, yet they seem strangely comfortable.

"Enough of this," you say. "Everyone out! All of you get in front and pull. I'll sit in the wagon and ride for a while."

So out they jump, some on one side, some on the other, some in front and some in back. They start pulling and the wagon starts jerking around but doesn't move in any definite direction.

"Wait a minute," you tell them. "We've got to work together here. Let's get these harnesses hitched up together and all start pointing in one direction."

And they do. The wagon starts to move. But once in a while one of the horses decides to pull in a different direction, or one can't seem to keep up. You find you can't just sit in the back. You need to be up in the driver's seat, holding the reigns. Hold them too tightly or give conflicting tugs and after a while the horses stop moving in frustration and confusion. Let go of the reigns and there is no way to predict where the wagon will end up. Apply the whip ferociously and you'll find all your best horses break free to hitch up with someone else. Don't apply it at all and you'll find even your best horses eventually matching the pace of the slackers.

Like any good analogy, this one will fall apart if pushed too far. However, a few clues will tell you why it's hard for business leaders to create the kind of cohesive, effective team so essential to doing business today.

Why is the leader in the harness?

Why is the owner or entrepreneur out front, pulling so hard? The answer is simple: Because that's exactly where he or she wants to be. This is especially true of companies that have grown from bootstrap operations. The entrepreneur has done it all, knows how to do just about everything, and has found that only by continuous exertion and will power will anything of any consequence ever get done. The owner is used to it, likes it, and likes the feeling of accomplishment and ego gratification this situation creates.

I have heard highly successful entrepreneurs complain bitterly about their management teams, their inability to get good people and the fact that they can't seem to get people to think for themselves. Yet it soon becomes obvious that they would just as soon no one think for themselves. They really want to do the thinking. They want to be the ones to make it all work. They want to be the Joe that makes the machine go. To admit that they are not the only ones capable of making the decisions, concluding the big deals, or cranking up the workforce would be a blow to the ego. It would call into question their indispensability.

So if you are an entrepreneur and you've ever felt you were pulling while others were just along for the ride, look first to yourself. Take a good, hard, long look. How would it feel if others were actually making most of the major contributions to the business? How would it feel if you went home at night knowing that others have done the work better than you were capable of doing? How would it feel knowing that you could let go and the business could keep right on going? If these thoughts make you queasy, you're probably in the harness, because that's exactly where you want to be.

One thing I should say about the leader in harness before I take a lot of flak. Some of you might be thinking, "The leader's got to be in harness, too. What about providing a good model? What about being out there working with the troops?"

Absolutely right. Times will come when you need to put the harness on and show those workhorses how to really pull. But if you're out there pulling and no one is driving, the horses won't know where they're going. They won't know that anyone knows or cares about where they're going.

Maybe the analogy starts coming apart here, but as a leader you've got to know when to be out in front pulling and when to be in the driver's seat steering. As we'll see in a moment, the real danger comes if you've been driving and you climb down in a way that invites the horses back into the wagon.

Why are the horses in back?

There are two types of horses and therefore two answers to this question. (In reality, of course, there are many more than two types, but we're trying to keep this simple, right?) For the first type of horse, the reason they are in the wagon is because that is exactly where they want to be and nothing will really change that. For the second type, they'd much rather be out in front pulling, but there are other things they want even more — like keeping their jobs.

To be completely honest, that there are two types of horses was a hard lesson for me to learn and I'm still stumbling on this one. Like most others, I tend to have the idea that most people are pretty much like me in how they think, react, desire or value. Thank God it's not true. (I can hear my wife and kids agreeing with that one!)

Some people just want a job. Others crave responsibility and the chance to show what they can do. Some people want to work, do a good job, pick up their pay-checks and go home. Some find their work a major focus for their life and others find it purely a means to an end.

Whether employees are in one camp or another doesn't say anything about their value, either as human beings or employees. Some of the most valuable employees whose performance is critical to the company may be those "job" people versus "career" people. In my experience, the work ethic tends to be stronger with "job" people than "career" people. Dependability is frequently without question. So it's important to understand I'm not saying one group is good and the other bad.

It's important to understand these two motivations, however. And when you're building a team and encouraging the workhorses into the harness it's important to know that different people want different things.

Considering there are two types, both may still end up in the back of the wagon — not pulling. With the first type, here's what you have to do. You go to them and say, "What I would really like you to do is get into this harness, pull really hard until quitting time and then go home and enjoy yourself." In other words, they need to be told what is expected of them and then allowed to do it. They will be as happy in the harness pulling as they were in the wagon riding. But what they very much need is clear direction and a good feedback system to know if they are doing what is asked of them.

The other group is never happy in the wagon. They'd like to be out in front pulling. They are more likely the potential leaders. If they're in the wagon, they are probably sulking about. They have a lot to contribute, a lot of energy, ideas and drive. Unfortunately, they do not feel free to contribute.

Many of these horses have been hired with the understanding that they should be out in front pulling. You're not happy to discover they're in the back; neither are they. How they got there and how to get them back out can be illustrated by this true story. (Some facts have been changed to prevent recognition.)

Why the horse climbed into the wagon.

A company hired an experienced manufacturing executive to bring on a higher level of management expertise and help it maintain its growth. The company had a number of long-time, key managers but hired this new person to become the supervisor. The owner-entrepreneur was a very strong-minded, controlling leader.

The new manager arrived with ideas, enthusiasm and a commitment to make the job work for him and his new company. At first everything went well. But when I met him and talked to him I recognized that he was in the process of crawling into the back of the wagon and I wondered what had happened. When I heard the story, I understood.

One of the new manager's first tasks was to review the organizational structure and each of the key managers, evaluate their performance and replace as needed. He went about the task carefully and thoroughly, and noticed considerable unevenness in the vice president's responsibilities. One long-time employee held the VP title, but neither his responsibilities nor his performance lived up to the expectation.

Our man talked to the VP, and they discussed revising his job description. Either he would accept these responsibilities as part of his job or he would continue with the work he was doing but without the VP title and requisite pay. The Veep went along, telling the new general manager that he would accept the new responsibilities.

Instead of actually accepting the change, however, the long-time employee complained to his good friend, the owner.

"I've worked long and hard for you," he told the owner, "and no one is more loyal. Then this new guy comes in here and none of that seems to count any more. I just want to know one thing. Who's running this company, you or that new guy?"

The owner squirmed, then honored the "end run" and told his old friend he would have a talk with the new manager. Following that talk, the long-time VP was told there would be no changes and the new manager started to crawl into the wagon. As he explained it to me, he had moved his whole family to town and needed this job to work out.

Good horses want to pull, but when told their contributions are counter-productive, unimportant or not valued, they will just go along for the ride.

However, the really good ones will only ride for a while. That new manager only lasted another six months before he found a different wagon. I hope for his and the new wagon owner's sake, that this guy is in a harness pulling hard.

Teamwork is the "Power and the Glory" of Friendship Marketing.

This is a book that says the heart of a business is building relationships. If your business is a one-person operation, you are the team. But for everyone else, the fact seems obvious that everyone involved in the business needs to be involved in the work of building relationships. But clearly it isn't obvious.

Let me give you one example. One of the best national ads using "Friendship Marketing" is the United Airlines TV spot with the executive meeting with his management group. The tone of the meeting is very serious, as if a calamity has just happened. The exec explains that a long-time friend and client has just fired the firm. It seems they had lost touch. Using the phones, faxes and everything else wasn't enough. He says the solution is to get back to face-to-face communication. A manager objects: "But we've got clients in over two hundred cities!" And the seasoned boss starts handing out airline tickets. Some brave soul asks him, "And where are you going?" He answers, "To visit that old friend who fired us this morning."

It's a great ad and represents some fundamental principles of Friendship Marketing very well. So what's the problem? The problem is that the reputation for "friendly skies" seems to have pretty well died. A former steward for the airline who still flies frequently says she never chooses United. Why? According to her, the service is too awful.

If you are the owner or manager of your enterprise, you can't do Friendship Marketing alone. You can't build your business alone. You can't do much of anything without your team. What's more, all the good work of building solid, loyal relationships can be undone by a single thoughtless act. And employees in your company who subscribe to the ideas of Friendship Marketing or commit to identifying and building strategic relationships will give up if they don't see efforts made in every part of the organization.

Regis McKenna in *Relationship Marketing* agrees, saying that true marketing "has to be all-pervasive, part of everyone's job description, from the receptionists to the board of directors." And, says McKenna, that kind of marketing has to be genuine. According to him, "its job is neither to fool the customer nor to falsify the company's image. It is to integrate the customer into the design of the product and to design a systematic process for interaction that will create substance in the relationship."

The bottom line is this: If you decide to make relationship building the heart and soul of your enterprise, you are committed to building a team effort. The two cannot be separated.

That's what I mean when I say teamwork is the "Power" of Friendship Marketing. The resolve of everyone on the team is the motor that drives the machine. It is the compelling force. It's what moves things, makes them happen.

Teamwork is also the "Glory." In other words, the whole idea behind Friendship Marketing is that we find our purpose, meaning, and value as humans in the quality of our interactions and relationships with other humans. To make this work in a vacuum, without your co-workers, independently instead of corporately, would be totally contradictory. Making Friendship Marketing happen in your workplace will be its own reward. The glory. Working together with a group of people who share goals and dreams is something we all want.

Peter Senge in *The Fifth Discipline* described the landmark experience of being on a good team. Whether in sports, drama or at work, we shared a common goal that was bigger than all of our individual goals. We trusted each other, added to each other's strengths and compensated for each other's weaknesses. Senge says the results are extraordinary. "I have met many people who have experienced this sort of profound teamwork," he said. "Many say that they have spent much of their life looking for that experience again."

The fact that creating a team has its own rewards is really a bonus. To produce results, the team is necessary. But even if it weren't necessary for the sake of performance, it would still be critically important because of what being a team member means to us. Creating a winning business that builds long-term, loyal relationships has economic rewards. Being part of such a team provides even more significant spiritual rewards.

Creating your team.

Let's say you're going to focus on building stronger relationships with the right few, and you recognize you can't do it alone. You need a team. How do you go about building that team? We can't pretend to be comprehensive here; there are dozens if not hundreds of books on this subject alone. But we can focus on a few critical elements of team building. We'll discuss how to define winning, identi-fy roles, overcome obstacles, and use Friendship Marketing principles to build your team.

First, define winning.

I have to apologize for the sports analogy. But I only apologize halfheartedly because the apology always seems to be directed at women I think ought to be insulted by the apology. After all, they're into sports virtually as much as men these days. Secondly, the word "team" itself is a sports analogy. If we talked about building an "army" we'd be using war analogies; if we talked about build-ing "community" we'd be using sociological analogies. We'll use team and we won't be apologetic anymore.

Teams are focused on winning, and winning teams understand what winning means. The most obvious problem when a company is having difficulty with building a team is that most of the players don't know what winning is. Chances are, they don't even know what game they're playing.

There have been several great business books comparing business to sports. They all ask: Why are people so reluctant to give work their all while during the weekend they play their hearts out at a game they really enjoy? The logical answers are the differences between work and play.

In games, especially team games, the team understands the game they are play-ing. They know the rules, they know what they have to do to win, and they have constant feedback from the scoreboard that tells them whether they are winning or losing. The writers of these books tell you that if you replicate the competitive nature of game playing in the workplace you will see productivity improve and your workers start acting like a team.

The most basic element in this approach is to define "winning." Since I am fre-quently asked to help with marketing and business development strategy I ask a question early on: What is your definition of winning? Perhaps you don't have a simple answer to that question either. That's understandable; defining win-ning is not necessarily easy. It demands a very high degree of clarity and focus. It demands simplicity.

The most popular games tend to be those where winning is easily determined and is immediately clear to everyone. The ones that require subjective judgment are more difficult to get really excited about. Synchronized swimming (which in my judgment is pretty darn subjective) lacks widespread crowd appeal. Even the very popular sports of ice skating and gymnastics are often frustrating to watch because the judges seem to use some sort of inside language or knowledge to make their subjective determinations. And then even politics get involved. Not so with basketball, baseball, soccer, football, hunting, or golf. You play the game by the rules and you win or lose. It's as simple as that.

Simplicity is the hardest thing, because simplicity demands saying no to pursuits that are valuable and worthwhile. So if your definition of winning fills several pages, it probably isn't going to work. And if it isn't clear, simple and obvious to you, it certainly isn't going to be clear, simple and obvious to your team.

What happens when a team doesn't have a clear sense of winning or losing? Everyone decides for themselves what is important. The good ones will dedicate their sincere efforts meeting the goals they think are most important. Maybe a great production manager heard you say that getting inventory figures down is the key to financial success. So he works hard and is very successful at just-in-time inventory and reducing costs — but at the price of stretching out delivery schedules. The sales department is screaming but he believes the company's financial future is more secure with lower inventory figures. He's playing his own game — and winning — while the sales people are playing a different game — and losing.

Winning has to address the big picture. You can win a series of downs in football and still lose the game. You can have a great quarter in basketball or hit a home run in baseball in a losing effort. You can win a great battle and lose the war. Certainly, short-term definitions of winning are valuable and might be just what is needed.

For example, you may determine that the company has to reduce its debt in order to position itself for growth. So you define winning as reducing the operating debt to x amount or x percent. The problem with short-term wins is they must continually be redefined. So, you accomplished that one, now what? After awhile, the team starts to think that playing this game is simply a matter of crisis management. Find a crisis and manage it. It's much better to define winning with the big picture in mind.

Defining winning for your team is very much a strategic effort (refer to Chapter 10 for a complete discussion of strategy and focus). So it must be big picture and it must be exceedingly clear and simple. It must also be specific to your company, your situation. What is winning for one company — even a competitor — may not be winning for you. It has to do with your company's particular competencies, the hopes and desires of everyone on the team, and the opportunities and obstacles that you face.

In our case, in our small company, we had some good discussions about this and decided winning consisted of answering three questions:

- Are our clients happy?

- Are we having fun?

- Are we making money?

We couldn't answer "no" to any of those three questions and remain content. If we were having fun and making money, but our clients weren't happy with us, we knew we wouldn't be making money and having fun for long. We might make our clients happy and be making great money, but if we weren't having any fun in the process, well, that isn't what we wanted either. It had to be all three.

Of course one of these three areas might be a little more out of whack than the others at any particular time. Then we know we have to make some adjustments. If we have to work a little harder, put in some extra time, make a little less money in order to make clients happier, then we'd better do that. But the idea is to get them all back into balance, not to create a permanent situation where one of those elements is dominant.

What is right for us, though, is not necessarily right for you, your company or your team. How you go about determining winning may help define your team building skills and approach. If you determine this is something only you can do and they'd better just go along with it, well, that's one approach. On the other hand, you could see your work as a collaborative effort. If you need others to define winning as much as they need you to help them find focus and clarity, you've probably got a lot better chance of creating a participative team.

Next, integrate team winning and individual performances.

The dynamics of an effective team are complex. A great team benefits from outstanding individual performances added together to create a performance greater than the sum of its parts. If the individual performances take precedence, the team suffers. At the same time, few teams can achieve greatness without outstanding individual performances. So you must reward individual effort and success without risking the cohesiveness of the team.

That brings us to three important subjects: measurement, recognition and compensation.

Measurement: A little scoreboard magic.

You've got to have a scoreboard. You've got to. Everyone on the team must be able to look up from the game once in awhile and check the score. The scoreboard lets the team know whether they are winning or not. This is so important and so defining, that I am convinced if you want to create a team, the place to start is by making a scoreboard. Doing so will force you to define winning, it will make clear what you are measuring, and it will provide the most powerful company-wide communication tool you can create.

The issue of group versus individual performance is highlighted in the scoreboard. The most important measurement is the team score, but individual scores matter as well. Look at the incredible fascination with statistics in sports. Every conceivable little thing is measured and every star performer is measured against the top stars of the game from the time the game began. On the job, individual stats are important to maximize productivity. And the more visible they are to everyone, the more of a motivational tool they become.

Public knowledge is an incredibly powerful force, too. Let me give you a quick example. Our Rotary club had an ongoing problem with attendance. We were generally in the bottom third of clubs in our district. So we had a mandatory speech from the current club president as a regular feature about twice a year. A little blip of inspired improvement followed and then it was back to the same pattern of tardiness. A particularly bright member suggested a new approach: Let's post the attendance figures for each member every week.

You might guess what happened. We got a copy of the table of the attendance percentages every week, and pow! We went from near the bottom to near the top of our district almost overnight. We could scan the list and see at a glance who was helping and who was hurting. Most of all, we could see where we were and I can tell you that I for one did not want to be responsible for dragging the club's attendance percentage down. We've never had a presidential speech on the subject since. The difference was simply the power of public information.

Put those productivity measures out there. Get it down to the smallest possible unit — down to the individual if at all possible. Let everyone know in the organization who is making real contributions and who is going along for the ride. If the team goal is important, the rest will take care of itself.

Recognition: More important than money.

Every study on the subject repeats the same simple truth — we are all motivated more by recognition than money. Yet how many businesses really understand this and use it to build an effective team? It's such a hard thing. As a boss you tend to pay attention to performance when it becomes a problem, not when it is contributing to your success. Kenneth Blanchard's greatest insight was this: "Catch somebody doing something right." Problem is, that it seems so much harder than catching someone doing something wrong.

Recognition is critically important, but I'm not sure that the typical organizational approach to recognition works all that well. Public pats on the back, little bonus programs and big awards dinners are all important and valuable. But I think the recognition that really counts comes from the team, not the coach.

I made a special point of looking out for this when the thought occurred to me. I watched the Seattle Mariners. (You know, since 1995 it's been okay to admit you're a Mariner fan). Lou Pinella is a pretty well-respected manager as far as I can tell. If his players don't love him, they certainly seem to respect him. So it would seem that recognition from him would be the important thing — a critical motivating factor. But what I observed, after a close and important game, is that players looked to each other for celebration and recognition. The relationships between team members became more important than those between the player and coach. The high fives offered by players such as Griffey and Buhner seemed to be the highest rewards, causing younger players to literally expand.

Sure, Lou was in the midst, a part of the team sharing in mutual congratulations. But he wasn't at the end of the line or at the front of the line. Just part of the group and no one seemed to look to him for anything more or anything less than the other players.

The real trick in building a team, then, is creating an atmosphere of mutual support, respect and recognition. An atmosphere where team members can look to each other. The managers, bosses, and supervisors are just part of the team, doing their parts.

How do you do this? By making teamwork and recognition a value. Start by asking the receptionist or another support person to point out to you when someone is making that individual effort that really counts. Then ask the receptionist to thank that person personally and let him or her know what it means to the company — and the receptionist personally. Do it all around the organization. Let everyone know that part of their job is cheering everyone else on. Put up a board in your office for kudos. Ask people in the organization if they've complimented anyone lately on a job well done. Then ask yourself the same question.

Compensation: The way to focus attention.

Your compensation program is like the two-by-four used by the mule trainer. It's a powerful tool for getting attention focused where you want. But take care. Misused or misapplied, it will do you a lot more damage than good.

We won't go into this subject here in depth. Instead, here are five simple ideas to help you evaluate whether your compensation program is performing the way you want it to.

Pay communicates what you really expect of your team.

Whether you intend it or not, how you pay your people communicates your priorities much more loudly than anything you say. This is especially true of bonuses or extra compensation awards. A commission structure tells them making the sale is important; it says nothing about customer satisfaction. Monthly salary or hourly wage tells workers that you want them selling you their time for whatever purpose you wish during the time period. Piece work pay tells them how much you value every piece they complete. Bonuses offered to managers and not line employees communicates that performance goals are up to the managers.

You get the picture. No matter what structure or pay method you choose, you communicate with it whether you mean what you are saying or not. In evaluating your pay system, try to understand what is currently being communicated and whether that is what you really want to be telling them.

Another way to look at this issue is this: If you decide to focus on one thing (market share, for example, or perhaps providing highest quality in your industry), then your compensation system ought to reflect that single-minded focus.

Link pay to individual performance and team performance wherever possible.

Bonus and performance-based pay is a real bugaboo of many business managers. Very few seem genuinely satisfied with what they have, but few can come up with something better. In my mind, the best compensation systems link individual pay to individual performance to the strongest degree possible.

However, the individual performance goals must be strongly linked to the team goals and there must also compensation for team performance.

The reason is simple. Strong performers are often motivated by competitiveness, ambition, or a desire to prove to themselves and others what they are capable of achieving. To bury that desire in a common pay structure does not offer these exceptional people the opportunity to excel and to be rewarded for their excellence. Frequently, the average workers will complain. But it seems to me they instinctively understand that the pay they receive for their average performances is covered in part by the excellent performance of the stars.

I've gone through the exercise with several different companies. Look at the labor costs of your production people overall. If they are paid on an hourly or monthly basis, they are paid for their time, not their performance. But some clearly outperform others. Put some numbers to it and you will find a few that are producing great numbers, a few that are clearly not performing adequately, and most that are somewhere in the middle. The labor costs have been set at the average.

If everyone performed at the highest level, they could be getting considerably higher pay — in some cases astoundingly higher pay. But they can't because the high performers have to, in effect, "pay" for the worst performers. By paying on the basis of performance, you will have some getting paid very well, much better than before, and others perhaps not able to earn a living wage.

What will happen? There's a good chance you'll end up with all superstars as the high performers in other competitive companies come to learn how you are doing things. The poor performers will look for work elsewhere — probably a place that pays hourly or monthly so their poor performance can be paid for by someone else's outstanding efforts.

There's another powerful reason to link pay to individual performance. Most people want to get credit and rewards for what they can control. It's great to get a company-wide bonus check based on the performance of the team, but an individual has so little control over what everyone else does.

Executives are often confused when team bonuses don't motivate. Yet it's easy to understand when you see someone who is motivated by the goal and puts in the extra effort — only to discover that co-workers are not thrilled by the team goal and won't put in the same effort for a promised reward. Soon the motivated ones realize that their future is not in their hands, but comes down to the weakest link in the chain. One or several people unwilling to play brings the whole scheme down. Staff who respond to bonuses and team goals are most likely to continue responding when they see a direct and immediate result in their own pay (don't forget recognition) based on what they themselves do.

Competitiveness today requires new approaches.

Time has drastically changed the way we all do business. And these changes don't come because small business owners or managers like you or me attend seminars, learn the latest trends and then go out and put these grand new ideas into practice. They come when people like you respond to opportunities and obstacles and figure you have to change to survive or thrive.

The changes I'm talking about here have to do with flexibility. We've all had to learn that if we don't keep our organizations in a state of ready change and adaptation, it doesn't take long to get caught in the backwash of some competitor. Nowhere is this more true than in dealing with the workforce. Workforce needs are exceptionally dynamic. At the same time, current employment laws and organized activities seemed designed to contradict the economic reality of flexible workforces — hence outsourcing, freelancing, temps, consultants and the small subcontractor.

Compensation systems today need to reflect the need for rapid change and flexibility. Team goals may change. Highly-structured and complex systems may become outdated before they can even be put into effect. Flexible cost structures, especially flexible labor costs, are a critical component to creating a flexible, adaptable organization. Compensation programs providing that flexibility, especially when tied to superior individual performance, are one of the strongest tools managers have to increase their competitiveness.

Match your pay system to your team's personal styles and aspirations.

Obviously every organization is different, and every work force is different. In small businesses, it's no surprise that the work force tends to reflect the personality and values of the management or entrepreneur. Makes sense, doesn't it? Likewise, pay systems ought to reflect the peculiar personality and aspirations of your work force.

We'll discuss this further when we cover alignment of goals as it applies to the team, but you should understand what your work force or team really wants. Is it growth, challenge or opportunity? Is it high pay, to meet some social group expectations or to live a lifestyle that demands an upper income? Is it to take care of families, prepare for college or buy an RV? Is it security, to know there will be a job and a decent retirement? Aspirations will be determined as much by demographics (age and sex) as by psychographics (personality and lifestyle issues).

In other words, don't create your compensation system in a vacuum. Understand the numbers — what labor costs can be allotted, for example. What percentage of profits can be set aside for performance bonuses? Once you have the basic parameters in place, call the troops in and have a good open discussion about how people want to get paid. The more they understand what the basic guidelines are, the more they can actively and fruitfully participate in the discussion.

For example, if they understand you've got to charge $29.95 for an oil change to remain competitive, they can then understand how much you can pay out for labor and still expect to stay in business. You need to know what those numbers look like and they should know as well. Some people call this "open book management." I think it's a terrific idea.

A marketing services firm with which I am quite familiar decided to employ these principles. Like many others in the advertising/public relations/promotion industry, business was subject to a lot of ups and downs. Really busy, then really slow. You hire when you get busy, then find yourself carrying a lot of overhead when you're not.

But the boss didn't like layoffs. For one thing, they never seemed to go over well with the layoffees. Finding and training replacement employees was a big pain and an expensive process, as well. Without layoffs, though, the boss watched profits melt away as soon as there was a slowdown. So the decision was made to go to a variable pay schedule.

With the exception of some administrative staff, every employee (including the boss) was put on a pay system completely tied to the individual employee's contribution to the company's revenue. The owner (me) decided what the maximum amount was that could be allotted to labor costs, then we divided the other basic categories into overhead and profit.

Then, given the maximum, the staff was asked how they wanted labor costs divided up. How much to medical benefits, retirement, vacation pay, sick leave; how much to people who were designers or writers but had no client development or relationship responsibility versus how much to those who had to spend time taking care of clients. After much consideration (during which time an incredible amount was learned about the business by everyone) a formula was reached.

The results, while not universally acclaimed at first, have spoken for themselves. Everyone knows what to focus on. The downtimes have been survived and along with the paltry paychecks came the reminder that there would be no lay-offs. Productivity positively zoomed, profits now were both real and sustainable, and have proven to benefit everyone by helping to provide substantially improved offices and working conditions.

A few employees have come and gone. Some of those who have gone have criticized an "unfair" pay system that didn't recognize their talents and contributions. But it also proved effective in attracting some powerful new talent who had the experience to know that the labor percentage offered was substantial and their ability to earn was totally in their own hands.

I must admit that the basic principles I derived about compensation have largely been driven by this experiment. But I can also say that I have seen it work. I have tried on numerous occasions to have other companies adopt a similar sort of strategy and have heard the many different reasons why "it can't be done." I remain unconvinced. More and more I am certain that the future of these companies will depend on creating compensation systems that attract and reward the highest performers and do not place a penalty on them to support those who can't or won't keep up.

1) Identifying roles: Recognize diversity.

There are very few teams where everyone plays the same role. Your team will also be made up of people with different tasks, duties, responsibilities and roles to play. In the past, these roles have been identified using two tried and true methods: the organization chart and job descriptions. These methods are still useful, but they're understood differently. Flexibility is the key. Ability to move and change quickly is critical. And an all-consuming focus on the strategic relationships of the company demands a new response to organizational concerns.

2) Which comes first, frontline or support?

Here's a different way to look at things. If you put your strategic relationships at the top of your organization chart, the people who deal directly with the customers appear right below the customers. Anyone who deals directly with the customer is considered "frontline." In the case of a fast food restaurant, that puts the workers behind the counter at the frontline. Everyone else's job in the entire organization is to support the work of the frontline. The frontline staff ought to want to get the burgers to the customer fresh, hot and well made. That's the job of the cooks.

But when a patron complains to a janitor that he or she can't find a clean table, that janitor is now on the frontline. The fate of the business, especially as it relates to that particular customer, is now totally and completely in the hands of that janitor. With a right response, loyalty is built. With a wrong response, everyone is hurt — from every cook and waitperson to the CEO in Chicago.

So here's how the new organization charts look:

Service Firm Organizational Chart

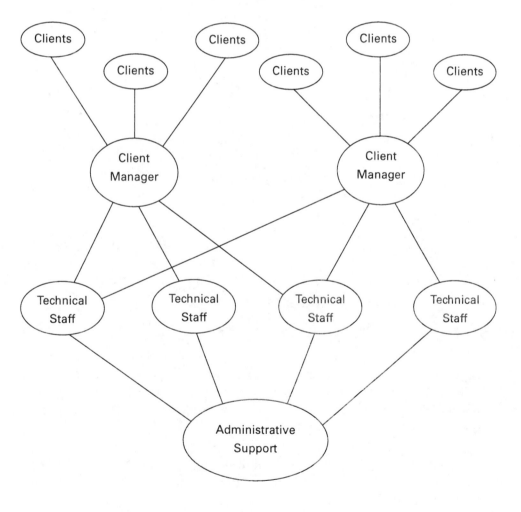

Manufacturing Organizational Chart

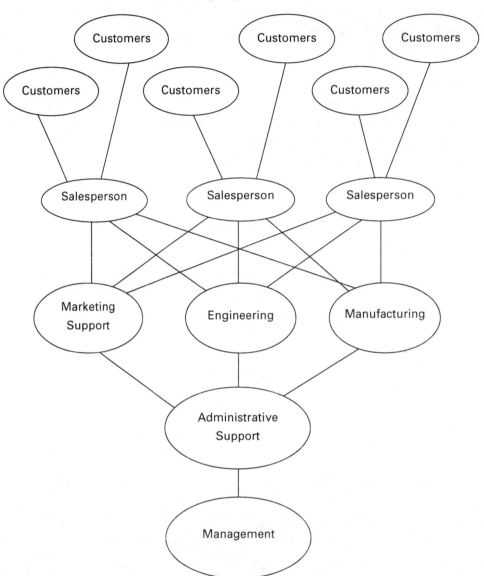

In reality, these charts are dynamic, flexible, fluid and always changing. At one time or another almost everyone might be frontline. (In fact, it's a good idea for those bigwigs in Chicago to get behind the service counter once in a while to understand the demands of caring for the customers.)

The picture should look like a football team receiving a kickoff. If the kick goes where it is expected, the team's best return man will run it back. The team is trained to support — provide the blocks that will give the runner the greatest chance of going the greatest distance. But if it's a short kick and the ball goes to one of the upmen, does the team say, "Hey, wait a minute, you're not supposed to get the ball. Give it to the right guy!" No, they quickly readjust their formation and block for the new ball carrier who, until a second ago, assumed he was one of the blockers.

One thing has become clear to me through many hard lessons: Not everyone ought to be trying to play the same role. We talked earlier about two kinds of horses. People have different comfort zones, different priorities, different ambitions, different personalities. I've spent way too much time trying to fit square pegs into round holes. If you are doing that, I can assure you no one will be particularly happy with the effort or the outcome. This is true of the type of job you ask people to do as well as the issue of frontline or support roles.

Since we take the view here that the value of a business is to be found in its relationships, it makes sense as a corollary that the most valuable people in the organization are those who are building customer relationships. That's why checkers in supermarkets are the highest paid, right? That's why flight attendants get more than executives, right? No, it doesn't work that way. But maybe it should.

In a recent book, *The One to One Future*, authors Pepper and Rogers suggest that employees ought to be compensated on the basis of the lifetime value of the clients or customers they manage. Interesting thought. What is the lifetime value of an airline passenger? Well, if that passenger is a frequent flier, or a person who influences the decisions of many others, then the lifetime value could be measured in the hundreds of thousands of dollars. Shouldn't the person or team who creates strong loyalty see some reward for their efforts?

One of the problems you will encounter with this concept is that not all will agree that their contributions ought to be measured on the basis of their connection to customer relationships. An outstanding engineer may believe he or she ought to be compensated for being an outstanding engineer and for making outstanding engineering contributions.

True enough. But if there is no connection between those contributions and customer loyalty, what exactly is the point? The engineer must understand precisely why those engineering contributions are important. That way, engineers will have a clearer sense of what they are doing, and a clearer understanding of the critical role that others (such as in marketing, manufacturing, and shipping, etc.) play in the engineer's success.

Dealing with obstacles helps maintain the team.

We've talked about winning, creating scoreboards, identifying different roles, and compensation systems that match priorities. All things are critical to create an effective team. Maintaining one is another matter.

Teams are destroyed from within. Nothing can really destroy a team from outside itself. Even defeat doesn't do it. Say the team doesn't win. The loss is usually still an outstandingly positive experience for everyone on the team if the integrity of the team is maintained. Defeat may exacerbate internal tensions and in so doing contribute to the demise of the team, but even this only proves that teams are destroyed from within.

Politics is usually the term used for the cancer that works on the inside of a team. But what is politics? Let's go back to Peter Senge's description of the great team experience. He says that a great team is characterized by a group whose common goals were larger than individual goals. This is an absolutely critical concept. Politics is a symptom of *personal* agendas. It occurs when individual goals supersede the team goals, when what one individual or group wants becomes more important than that which unites the team.

Knowing this enables you to deal effectively with the team-killing cancer of personal agendas. Understanding how unrelated personal goals that conflict with team goals can damage or destroy the team will help when you're initially selecting the team. Deal straight up with it. If there's a question at the outset, discuss it. "I understand that being appointed the Regional Sales Manager is very important to you, but I'm concerned it may lead you to downplay the contribution of others. That would damage the team. Are you willing to let that promotion come as it will and not let your desire for that stand in the way of giving credit where credit is due?"

Then, if the issue comes up, you've put the person on notice. You've also said that even though you recognize the personal objective as a legitimate goal, you will not tolerate the pursuit of that objective at the expense of the team working together well.

You cannot deal with it by telling someone her agenda or her goal ought to be abandoned. Personal goals are ultimately the most important to each individual. But individuals must be able to see how operating within the team is the best way to reach those personal goals. The slugger who refuses to bunt to move a base runner may very well find his opportunities limited, to say nothing of the lack of support he will get in the clubhouse.

What happens when it becomes clear that a personal goal simply won't fit within the team goals? Or a team member steadfastly refuses to subjugate his or her desires to the team goals? You've got three options:

1. Let the team disintegrate (not a preferred option).

2. Replace the team member (after giving every opportunity to get things straightened around).

3. Let the team take care of it.

Here's what I mean by "letting the team take care of it." A management retreat I conducted had "team building" as a major theme. It gave me the opportunity to test some of my theories about teams and how they work. There were about twenty-four people — mostly management types. I divided them into three groups of eight each. Each team was given a picture puzzle with the same number of pieces and the game was to see who could put the puzzle together first or get the closest in the fifteen-minute time frame. Since we were at a ski resort, the prize was a crazy snowboard hat.

Here's where it got interesting. I had prepared different roles for each member of the team and these were selected at random. No one on the team was to know what the roles of the other team members were; each was given role instructions independently. For example, there was a "leader" who was to take charge, get things organized. Except, of course, no one knew who the designated leader was.

There was also the "leader wanna be." The instructions for that person were to try to take over authority from anyone else who appeared they might be trying to lead the group. Then there was the "enabler" whose job it was to try to help out and be nice to everyone to the point of being annoying. There was the "engineer" who always felt he/she had a better way of doing things. Whatever was suggested, that person was to suggest a different way.

One of the most interesting roles was "obstacle." This person's role was to do whatever he or she could to keep the team from winning, but do it without getting caught. And, of course, no one knew what the other team members' roles were.

So the game began. What a ruckus! It showed me for one thing that winning is important. These people went at those puzzles with a ferocity that was amazing. It wasn't the stupid snowboard hat that was motivating them. It was the game, the competition, winning.

Remember, all the roles were chosen at random. It so happened that on one team the role of "obstacle" was drawn by a sweet and exceptionally helpful young administrative assistant. In real life, this person would do just about anything to help the team. In real life, an enabler — in this game, the obstacle. Since I was the only one in the room who knew what was really going on with the roles, I watched in amazement as "Mary" did her work.

While the team was frantically engaged in trying to put the puzzle together, Mary was quietly slipping pieces off the table and onto the floor. In the course of a few minutes she had eight or ten pieces under her feet. Now the game was going in earnest, time was ticking down, and the pressure was building. One of the team members noticed that a piece seemed to be missing. Then others began to notice. Mary innocently worked ahead on the puzzle.

Suddenly someone looked under the table and saw the missing pieces. "Hey, here they are! They're under Mary!" She feigned great surprise and the game went on, but now there was some suspicion. When Mary thought it safe again she spirited another piece off the table, but this time she was caught.

"Mary!" someone yelled. "You're taking the pieces." She denied it, but the suspicion was now great. Seeing her duty was to foil them and the game was coming near the end, she got bolder and grabbed a piece to drag it onto the floor. But now they took action. Mary, protesting loudly, was elbowed away from the table. "Get her away from here!" someone shouted — the leader or leader wanna be. As sweet and helpful as she was in real life and as much as she protested now, there was total agreement that the team could not afford to have her anywhere near the puzzle pieces. She was abruptly and physically separated from the team. With the obstacle removed from the game, the team went on to victory.

The team that wants to win will remove its own obstacles. That was the critically important lesson for me. If a team is truly focused, if it wants to win, if individual agendas are subjugated to the objective of the team — the team will take care of itself. As a result of this, when I confront politics at work, in my own situation or that of my clients, I conclude that the real problem is lack of clarity of goal or purpose. The team doesn't understand the game they are in, or doesn't understand what it will mean to them to win. If they truly understand that, the obstacles will be removed.

Using SALT helps to build the team.

We're going to come full circle. We said at the beginning of this chapter that you can't do Friendship Marketing on your own. You need a team. It's ironic that the very principles of Friendship Marketing that your team needs to build your business are the very same principles needed to build your team.

Strategic relationships.

This is more true of a larger team than a smaller one. Every group has influencers. If you need to mold a group of twenty or twenty thousand into an effective team, you need to know who the influencers are. If you cannot succeed in getting them to adopt the team goals and subjugate other personal or group goals, then your team will not succeed. You will not win the numbers game if you do not have the influencers with you.

Alignment of goals.

We've already dealt with this critically important subject in a variety of ways in this chapter. Defining winning, having team goals a priority, compensation that meets individual and group needs — all these are part of aligning goals. I am convinced that the reason so many managers have a tough time creating effective teams has to do with the fact that they expect the whole team to align their goals with the company's or the manager's.

Try turning it around. Knowing that a clear understanding of winning is critically important, how about asking the team how they define winning? How about getting a clear understanding of what they really want, what is important to them, what their aspirations are, before coming up with the team goals.

Growing your business to satisfy your own need for challenge and adventure may be important to you. But if your team places a higher value on security and stability, and you ask them to take the risks with you that more challenge demands, you may find yourself out in front with only a half-hearted team behind you. Your goals and their goals must be aligned. And the way to start the alignment process — just like with customers — is to find out from them what they really want.

Listening.

How do you find out what is important to your team? How do you know whether the influencers, the strategic relationships, are going to be pulling along with you? Listen. This strikes me as an unusual strategy. The new thinking is that businesses ought to listen more to their customers. Listen more to their employees? I'm not sure that idea has really hit yet.

But how can you build a team without it? You cannot show how the team can accomplish its goals if you don't know what those goals are, or what is really important to that team. Funny thing, you probably can't find out who the influencers are without listening as well.

"Lead with your ears," my friend and colleague Steve Hortegas likes to say, quoting from a contemporary version of the Bible. It's great advice for managers as well as marketers. If you want to build a powerful, cohesive team focused on winning, lead with your ears. Start by listening and discover the ways you can serve their aspirations rather than expecting them to serve yours.

Teamwork.

Use teamwork to create a team? It's starting to feel like we're looking into a series of mirrors. Assuming I'm speaking largely to control-freak type entrepreneurs who like to prove that they can do it all, one of the hardest things to learn is to let go and let others do it. "Leadership hates a vacuum," I like to say. Which means if a real vacuum exists, the real leaders will fill it.

Unfortunately, you don't always know who the real leaders are because you are too busy filling up vacuums. That's what makes you a leader; that's why you are at the head of your company or your group or your organization. You've seen those vacuums and you headed for them like water running downhill. It's natural to you. What's not so natural is intentionally letting vacuums exist to see who might step in.

A company had a strong operations manager, but it needed managers at the third level to step up and take more responsibility. The company needed more leaders, but whenever specific names came up for promotion or to take on more responsibility, the operations manager always said, "They're not ready yet. They just haven't learned enough."

It turned out the operations manager, a control-freak himself, didn't want anyone else to take responsibility. When the logjam was finally broken by the operations manager leaving, suddenly all those third level managers who weren't ready had to be ready and stepped up nicely to the new challenges. They never had the chance to grow and to show what they were capable of because the operations manager would allow no vacuums to exist.

You can't do it all; you can't even do it best. It's just your ego that's trying to convince you all the time that you can. Let it go and let the team win.

*"Some people wanted champagne and caviar when
they should have had beer and hot dogs."*
— Dwight D. Eisenhower

8

Selling:
It Helps to Have Friends

*The personal sales situation provides the greatest opportunity for developing key
relationships, yet it also carries the greatest risk of abuse. This chapter offers
sales training with service at its heart. Practical examples provide the
illustrations that demonstrate how building business and building
relationships are not opposites, but can and should be integrated.*

Chapter summary:

- Selling Basic One: People have needs.
  - The photocopier sale: How to untangle the need.
    1) Do the end run only as a last resort.
    2) Try to maintain direct contact without threatening the middle.
    3) Make the person in the middle your friend.
  - Tuning in to needs: Developing your antenna.
- Selling Basic Two: You can either meet those needs or you can't.
- Selling Basic Three: Find the ones whose needs and ability to pay match your
  ability to supply.
  - Finding suspects, prospects, customers.
    1) Suspects: Names on a list.
    2) Prospects: Faces with a name.
    3) Customers: Future friends.
  - Saints, sinners and savables.
- Selling Basic Four: Show them you have what they want.

- Never let them see you sweat.
- Match the style.
- Be briefer than you think.
- Address the needs directly.
- Don't hide anything.
- Ask for the order.
- Know the next step in advance.
- Be gracious — win or lose.
- Make it hard to say no.

You'll find plenty of sales training books at nearly every public library or good bookstore, filled with all kinds of great ideas about how to sell. The best ones will tell you that you need to give the people you are selling what they want. You'll do well if you follow that kind of basic advice.

But giving the customers what they want is not the traditional idea of selling. A good salesperson, some say, can sell a refrigerator to an Eskimo. A better salesperson will sell one with an ice maker. In other words, such a salesperson can convince otherwise intelligent people to spend money on things they don't really need.

Unfortunately, such people are not sales professionals, they are con artists. Selling, real selling, is the process of demonstrating how a product or service can meet specific needs. Nothing more or less.

Selling is remarkably easy when you look at it this way:

1. People have needs.

2. You can either meet those needs or you can't.

3. Find the people whose needs and ability to pay match your ability to supply.

4. Show them you have what they want, and everyone is happy.

Almost every problem in selling occurs because some part of this simple sequence goes awry. And unfortunately, selling problems happen often. Ethical problems, when the salesperson knowingly tries to create a false need. Effectiveness problems, when the salesperson isn't careful to understand the potential customer's real needs. And frustration, when the sales person finds that he or she has spent a lot of time trying to meet the needs of those one who aren't even the ones who will buy. (Or if they are, sometimes they don't have the money. That can be just as frustrating.)

The problems are virtually endless. The solutions can be found by breaking down each of our four selling basics.

Selling Basic One: People have needs.

Think about it. There are several billion people on this planet. You have something to sell. Out of all these people, there are probably hundreds, perhaps thousands, maybe even millions who need what you are selling. It's really quite encouraging.

If you conclude that this isn't true, take a closer look at your product or service. See if it can't be modified to generate more interest. People need flowers and exotic fruits, backrubs and bicycles. They need tweezers and recipe card holders and floor sweepers and jet leasing services. They need food for their bodies, minds and souls. The needs are endlessly varied, as fascinating as the people themselves, because individual people in one sense are neediness on two legs. The funny thing is, the more wealthy people are, the more needy they seem to become.

When you understand that there are many, many people who are looking for exactly what you have to offer, you will have a moment to relax and enjoy the thought. But only a moment. After that, you realize that the tough part is finding those needles in the haystack of Planet Earth.

Of course, finding them is what this book is mostly about. You've probably already read how to locate new business in previous chapters. If you skipped ahead to this one, I'll give you a hint: Your future success will most easily be found in your past success. In other words, look first at who you already know. The quickest treasure (though not necessarily the best) will be found there.

You should not assume, however, that just because people have an obvious need, you can meet that need automatically and easily. There are several reasons why not.

To begin, usually it's not possible to identify just a single need. People are more complicated than that, and they usually come with such a complicated web of those needs that it takes a near genius with the insight of a psychiatrist to separate real needs from wants from just wishes. If only it were as simple as Santa's list.

Then there's the small matter of competition. Market reality. No matter how good your idea, there's a very good chance a dozen or maybe a thousand others are just as convinced as you are that they have the answer to the needy one's prayers. But let's not worry about the competition for now. Let's stick with the factors you can control.

The photocopier sale: How to untangle the need.

Consider yourself lucky if you can direct your sales efforts at just one decision maker. Because as soon as more people get involved in a buying decision — and they generally always do — the process of identifying and responding to needs multiplies exponentially. Here's a simple example.

Let's say you want to sell a high-end photocopier to the largest real estate firm in town. The company is big, fast-moving, aggressive and has an enviable reputation. So you're having dinner at a friend's house, a social gathering for those involved in a community fund-raiser. During pre-dinner conversation you find yourself talking to the owner of the real estate company, Mr. Crow.

Of course he asks what you do and you tell him you represent Miraculous Photocopiers. By golly, he says, he's about to throw out his old photocopier. Seems the machine keeps breaking down and besides that, he's heard of a new machine that will actually print from everyone's computers on a network. That, he says, would be great and really save his busy salespeople some time and money.

Prudently you decide now is not the time to tell him your Miraculous copiers not only have the best reliability record on the market, but this is the company that just announced the new network copier system. Instead, you tell him you have something that might interest him and ask if you could call for an appointment. After getting his hearty assurances you get back to your wine.

The next day you make your phone call. You identify yourself as being from the Miraculous Copier Company and ask for Mr. Crow. You are told Mr. Crow is not available and the photocopier decision is in the hands of Ima Powerhouse, the office manager. You explain you talked to Mr. Crow but you are told he has instructed that all calls about the photocopier be directed to Ms. Powerhouse.

With a sigh, you ask if you can talk to her and the call goes through. Through to her administrative assistant Jimmy, that is. Jimmy explains that Ms. Powerhouse is pre-screening proposals with a three-page questionnaire and would you like one sent to you? No, you say. You wish to talk to Mr. Crow. Obviously that's the wrong thing to say as Jimmy quickly reminds you by his tone of voice who is in charge. You backtrack. You'd love to fill out a stupid form.

We'll make a long and familiar story quite short. Mr. Crow in two minutes told you his needs. You know you have the solution to those needs. But you have to run a gauntlet to get to Mr. Crow, and that represents an entirely different challenge. As it turns out, the secretary and the office manager have needs, too. Their needs are usually not the same as Mr. Crow's, either.

Mr. Crow has his eye on the bottom line and what will do the most to help the business. Ms. Powerhouse, on the other hand, may need to prove her worth. She may wish to prove to someone in the office that she is capable of being very tough on suppliers. She may want to show she can save the company money. She may need to avoid problems in her family and so toss the business to her husband's third cousin.

You see the dilemma. The owner's or top executive's personal interest is often so closely aligned with the overall business performance that you can see a direct link between their needs and what is right for the business. That's not to say that a top exec may not also have more basic needs for things like acceptance, ego gratification and respect. It's just that these needs are often so imbedded in the company's bottom line.

But dig down a layer in the company and everything may start to change. By the time you reach Jimmy, several layers down, the needs often bear no resemblance to what is best for the business.

Several layers down, personal needs and goals almost always become primary. The mid-level person's agenda is normally: How is this going to help me (protect, advance, solidify) my position with the company and/or my boss? Sometimes the need is simply to prove to themselves or others that they are capable and that they have power. Seeing this at work is seldom pretty and very often extremely frustrating — especially if you remember that the business and the top decision makers have other, more pressing needs.

Nothing in my business career has caused me to make more mistakes than this dynamic. Certainly nothing has caused more frustration. And I've come to believe that the ability to sniff out and respond to different needs of different people in different positions within a customer's organization is one of the sales professional's most valuable skills. It's also one of the most difficult skills to acquire.

If the scenario I just described resembles sales situations where you might find yourself, you have a couple of choices. Learn to create your success in this difficult environment, or find a sales situation where you only have the end user to deal with. If you need to make the multi-tiered decision system work for you, here are a few suggestions:

1) Do the end run only as a last resort.

You may be tempted to bull your way through to Mr. Crow by calling him directly, sending a letter or volunteering to caddy the day he's on the golf course. Resist the temptation unless you have tried everything else. If not, you'll burn your bridges. If you make the end around and you get turned back (Mr. Crow says, "Thanks for the information, but Ms. Powerhouse is the one you need to talk to,") you're as good as dead. Admittedly, desperate times call for desperate measures; just make certain you understand the risk.

2) Try to maintain direct contact without threatening the middle.

I asked an experienced salesperson once how he dealt with the power person in the middle syndrome. This was the same person I had watched sell an expensive computer system by simply asking questions, so I had a lot of respect for his sales expertise.

"I always start at the top," he told me, "with the president." Frequently he was directed to the "appropriate" person in the organization, but only at the suggestion of the boss. That way, he could tell Ms. Powerhouse that "Mr. Crow asked that I give you this information. He felt it would be of use to you in your decision because of...."

Then, he continued to keep the boss informed of the process. He documented the sales process and sent a copy to the CEO. That way he kept the power people straight and honest. They would know that someone was looking over their shoulder.

Of course, selling from the top down is a delicate game. There's a risk of causing the same kind of alienation as the desperate end around. However, if you are careful in how you do it and open in your explanations to the person in the middle, this process can help protect you and actually help everyone involved. The success of this technique largely depends on whether you also follow the next suggestion.

3) Make the person in the middle your friend.

If you clearly understand the goals of the power person in the middle, and you make it a standard practice to align with your customer's goals, you may find yourself making a friend. The middle person's goals may be different than the boss's, but that doesn't mean you can't accomplish them all. Think this through carefully, however, because there may be a price to pay in developing this complicated web of relationships.

Remember that the needs of the power person in the middle are frequently less connected to the business bottom line and more closely related to a personal bottom line. So if their job is important to them, they want to know how they are doing. And they want to know that whatever they do will make them look better to the boss — or at least help them avoid looking worse. In other words, expect them to take credit and avoid blame.

If you come along with something to sell, they will ask: If I pass this on with my recommendation, what are the chances that I can take credit for the success? And if it flops, what are the chances I'll be stuck with the blame?

Here's where it gets tough, because you may find that to meet this person's need, you will have to forgo credit that normally would fall to you. I never said this was logical. And — get ready for this — you may also have to position yourself to take the fall if things don't work out. Even if it's clearly not your fault.

Some people simply cannot do that. Others do it with such ease, make the sales and look mighty good in the process. Inevitably, your own ego and pride will work against you if they are pitted against someone else's ego and pride. Something's got to give, and if you don't, the thing to give will be the sale.

Tuning in to needs: Developing your antenna.

In the chapter on listening I mentioned that ears are the most important tool of the sales person. Let me amend that a bit. Ears must be hooked into the brain network to create a highly sensitive antenna, and this brain/ears combination is essential to the top notch salesperson.

Admittedly, it's a very difficult system to create if you didn't come by it naturally. Other than the right genes, I'm convinced that the best way to develop this antenna is through pure terror and desperation.

During the days when I was getting my business off the ground, I developed a habit of scanning the streets whenever I was walking or driving around. Since I often had no idea where the next paying job was coming from, I was looking for opportunity. Searching for potential customers. For some idea or suggestion that would trigger a reason to call on someone I knew or give me courage and enthusiasm to call on someone I didn't know.

When another business owner said he was like a coyote looking every which way for his next meal, I knew exactly what he meant. Hunger creates this. Lean, mean hunger. I've seen it in people who had seemed calm and laid back in sales jobs where they had a base and a good list of business. The change came on them when they switched to an entrepreneurial situation where their neck was on the line and business had to be developed. They developed that coyote look.

I've also seen it in employees when the safety net has been finally and ultimately removed. A change occurs. They're on their own.

I wish there were an easy way to create this antenna, but if there is I don't know of it. I do know that if more people developed a real sensitivity to the business needs around them, much less money would be spent on advertising and promotion and other inefficient means of developing business. A business with a whole staff of coyotes is a lean, mean, hungry and growing business.

Selling Basic Two: You can either meet those needs or you can't.

Even though there are a vast number of people right now who need exactly what you have to sell, many more of them don't need it. Given that reality, selling isn't nearly so much persuading as it is finding. As you probably know, however, finding those right few can be difficult, time consuming and frustrating. And since sales have to be made, shortcuts are taken. Usually the shortcut is ignoring whether or not the potential customer really needs what you are selling.

That's why salespeople have developed such a negative reputation. The old image tells us that if you are successful at selling things people don't need, then you must be a very talented sales professional. Truth is, keep ignoring the customer's real needs and your business career will be short and ignominious.

If you're clever, you may be able to meet sales quota goals for a time by goading, pressuring or lying. But you can't build friendships that way. Sell a junker car to a friend, forget to tell him about the sawdust you put in the oil to keep the noise down, and see how long your friendship lasts. Putting your own need to make a sale ahead of your customer's or your friend's need not to be abused is a certain way to lose all valuable relationships and eventually your career in sales.

Still, if you're sitting in front of an important customer, you naturally want to make the sale. You need to make the sale. But the only question that counts is: Can I meet his or her need?

The question seems deceptively simple, though the answer is daunting. Yes, there are people out there with needs you are uniquely suited to fill. They have the money and the willingness to pay to have those needs met. Problem is, it takes searching and listening to find them. It takes sleuthing and following all promising leads. It takes finding the needle in the haystack.

Obviously, that kind of work can be difficult, time-consuming and highly frustrating. The temptation will arise to take a shortcut. The most common one is to stretch your definition of what you supply. Ask a traditional salesperson why he is not meeting quotas, and he'll tell you that marketing won't adjust the pricing, or engineering won't design to meet customer demands. Salespeople want products and price points that will meet every sales situation they encounter.

Marketers instinctively understand you can't be all things to all people, but the traditional salesperson wants to argue: Why not, if I can get the commission? On the other hand, highly productive salespeople have a knack for determining very quickly how well their offerings match the customer's needs. If the match isn't there, they move on until they find that match.

The goal, then, is finding a good fit between what you supply and what the customer really needs. And if you are going to find a good fit, these four conditions need to be met:

1. The customer is buying for the right reasons, not to get you off his or her back.

2. The product will deliver or the service will perform as promised.

3. The investment was justified. Benefits to customers will be valued higher than the cost.

4. Happy customers will think highly of you and recommend you in the end.

If you can't meet these four conditions, then don't sell, not even if people want to buy. Not even if they are begging you. Why? It'll bite you in the end. An unhappy customer isn't worth the sale now. Everyone, they say, knows 250 other people. While they're unlikely to say anything if they are happy with you, you can bet that if they're unhappy most of those 250 (plus their friends and neighbors) are sure to hear about it.

Selling Basic Three: Find the ones whose needs and ability to pay match your ability to supply.

The first step to selling was recognizing the vastness of opportunity. The second was understanding the limits of that opportunity. Now the third step is work, and your job is to find the right match. The needle is in the haystack. In fact, many needles. But, oh, so much hay.

This basic step, then, is about finding. And to find the right customers, marketing and sales people tend to break people into categories. Two ways of categorizing may be helpful in the finding process.

Finding Suspects, Prospects, Customers.

In this categorization, people can be divided into four groups. (The fourth unmentioned category is "Neither," so naturally we'll concentrate on the first three.)

1) Suspects: Names on a list.

A Suspect is simply someone you think might become a prospect, and this is a category defined by temporary ambiguity. The problem is that either you or the suspect has limited information.

Your information may be limited because you don't know enough about them. What are their needs? Do their needs match your ability to supply? What is important to them? Can you help them achieve their goals? Can they afford what you're going to offer them? Until you find out those things, they must remain classified as Suspects.

They may also be Suspects because their information is limited. Do they know what you do? Do they understand what you can do for them? Do they have wrong information or wrong impressions? Do they think the solution is too expensive when a financing plan would meet their needs? If they don't have the information they need that tells them you may be able to help them, then they must remain Suspects.

Your first goal is to help Suspects become Prospects, which is done primarily by asking questions and following the 80/20 rule (described in Chapter 3 as listening 80 percent of the time and speaking only 20 percent). But beware — the most common mistake made here is to try to push a Suspect directly into being a Customer. Don't skip the Prospect stage, even if it seems like a shortcut. You'll find that your work will be easier and you'll gain more customers in the long run if you stay with the right order. Determine to help Suspects become Prospects first, then Customers.

For most selling, this process requires a face-to-face meeting. A common mistake is attempting over the telephone or by mail or e-mail what can only be reasonably accomplished face to face.

2) Prospects: Faces with a name.

A Prospect can answer yes to these two questions: First, can the person trying to sell me something actually meet my needs? And second, can I afford to pay the price?

If he or she can't answer yes to both questions, the "None of the above" category applies — unless their answer is "not yet." It's possible that some could remain prospects when their financial condition is likely to change and the price could be paid in the future.

3) Customers: Future friends.

A Customer is a former Prospect who not only can pay for the product or service, but definitely will. The important thing about this category for the salesperson is that this is not the end of the process, but rather the beginning. Now (and only now) you can begin to have a relationship that will mean something.

Liken it to a relationship between a man and woman. The Suspect phase is surveying the field. You separate the "possibles" from the "no ways." The Prospect stage is the wooing stage. Courtship is under way, with all its intricacies, stresses, ups and downs. But the Customer is the bride or bridegroom. Stepping from Prospect to Customer is the wedding and honeymoon. Now the relationship can blossom. Now love can take root.

If this is not your view of the Customer, if you're more of a "one night stand" sales person, take a good, hard look at your relationship building. Are you getting a lot of referral business from satisfied customers? Are you finding more and more business opportunities from existing, valued customers? Are you surprised when you find out from someone else that a customer you assumed was completely satisfied has been saying less than complimentary things about your product or service?

It's pretty easy for Customers to understand what being a Customer is all about. They've made their commitment, they've pledged to pay or they have already paid their money. Now it's time to deliver, and they're waiting to see if all the promises made in the courtship be fulfilled. Will delivery be on time? Will the process be smooth? Will the product perform as specified? As promised? And will questions, concerns or complaints be handled with the same promptness and responsiveness after the sale as they were before?

Answers to those questions will help define the true character of the salesperson and the company. Performance will help plant the seeds of confidence. And if a problem occurs, your willingness to put the bride or bridegroom first (and your interests second) will bring real loyalty.

Saints, Sinners and Savables.

This is the second method of categorization used when you need to find the right people. It's an exceptionally handy tool to use to check whether your efforts are strategic — that is, whether you are focusing your time and energy where they will do the most good.

The "S, S & S" technique is often used in political strategizing, so let's look at it in use there. Let's say you are a candidate for mayor on the Republican ticket and you have just one opponent, a Democrat. You will find there are voters who will always vote Republican and those who will always vote Democrat, no matter who is on the ballot. As a Republican you are certain you will get those base Republican votes, as certain as you will not get the base Democratic vote. The base Democratic voters (in this case) are the sinners and the base Republican voters are the saints. That leaves the savables. Since you can do nothing to affect the choices of the Saints and Sinners, it makes sense to work only on influencing the Savables.

Of course, the same principle works in selling. Let's say you are selling used Ford tractors. Some people won't buy a Ford anything, let alone a tractor. Sinners. Some people are only looking for new tractors. Sinners. A lot of people don't need tractors at all, new or used. Sinners.

There are, however, a number of people in town who will only buy used Ford tractors. You are certain of that. You have a lock on that market. Saints. Take care of them, of course. But don't count on them for business growth. That leaves the savables. Those would be the people who, under the right conditions, would consider buying a used Ford tractor. If you know who they are, it would be logical to focus most of your business development efforts on them.

Knowing about Saints, Sinners and Savables doesn't make locating the needle in the haystack an easy job, but it should make it easier. And it should also make it less painful. Selling, after all, is a studied process in pain avoidance. That's why the common complaint about salespeople is, "Oh, they're just order takers." Understand, it's much less painful to take orders from people who want your product than to take the risk of trying to convince someone who isn't sure.

Once you know that "finding" is the tough work of selling, the rest becomes much easier. Sales training professionals have their own ways of dealing with this. Some say, "It's just a numbers game." Talk to enough people and the numbers will work in your favor. Others have gone so far as to predict how many closings they will get out of how many contacts. When someone says "no" to them, they still say "thank you" because now they are one number closer to their closing.

Whatever the technique, remember that it's all pain avoidance. And it's all related to finding. Selling isn't so much about convincing as it is finding those people who have a genuine need for what you have to offer and an ability and willingness to pay for it. Once you have found those people, your only tasks are to present to them and make sure they clearly understand the benefits of what you are offering.

Selling Basic Four: Show them you have what they want.

Finally we come to the presenting part. The persuading part. The talking part. The part that most people think selling is all about. I hope you don't think that anymore.

If you do, please go back to page one and start over again. You can only effectively get to this part by careful listening and responding to what potential customers really need and want. If you don't know what they really need and want, how can you present it to them?

By the time you get to this part, which I normally call the proposal, the sale had better be 90 percent completed. You'll do best to make it short, sweet and simple, because that's what busy people want.

Unfortunately, in most cases sales people do just the opposite. They think their job is to sell. And that, they think, means boring someone to death with things that don't matter, or they bring up issues that no one cares about. You've probably been the subject of that kind of mistreatment.

There are many excellent books on making presentations, including standup presentations and written presentations. As we cover a few important highlights, recognize that there is much more to be said.

Never let them see you sweat.

In other words, be confident but not cocky. Some inexperienced presenters think it ingratiating to admit their nervousness up front. Not smart. Customer don't really care much about your feelings or your fears. In fact, they are only willing to give up their time because you have convinced them you have something that can help them. And since you've gotten this far, you had better communicate that you haven't wasted their time on a proposal you can't enthusiastically and confidently get behind.

Please remember this: You are not the point. What you have to offer, or the benefit of what you sell, is the only significant point. You need to become largely invisible. And you will do that by concentrating everything on your belief that the proposal you are presenting will produce the desired results.

So you still don't feel confident? Fake it 'til you make it. Be an actor. Just don't make yourself the show.

Match the style.

You will come to the point where you wonder about the best way to make your presentation to the customer. Written proposal? Informal discussion over the desk? Standup presentation with overheads? Video? Interactive? Internet? The choices are getting more and more numerous and complicated. The only safe way is to find out in advance what the client prefers.

Yes, that's easier said than done. If you haven't picked up the signals during your early interviews, check your antenna. And don't be quick to guess. Check it out. Ask around. Look for the signals. Above all, be prepared to be flexible, because presentation style is an indication of chemistry. If you haven't picked it up from your customer, he or she will likely sense that there just isn't a good match.

Be briefer than you think.

You've probably already picked this up by now, but let me make one point crystal clear. More sales are lost by too much talk than by too little talk. Most pitches are too long. Way too long.

Of course, you want to be complete and your customer wants you to be complete as well. But completeness does not normally mean exhaustive or exhausting.

Research reports of hundreds of pages normally have an "Executive Summary." At most the summary is a few pages; the best are a single page. Guess what part of the report executives read first?

Address the needs directly.

A good presentation normally has three parts, regardless of format.

a. Needs. This is where you say, "You told me you needed this," or "My research and analysis demonstrated that your needs are...." When you're in the needs stage you incorporate your listening skills most directly.

b. Solutions. The meat of the presentation, the part most people begin with, gives your solution to the need. You can think of the solution as the meat, but remember it's in a sandwich between needs and the next step. At this stage, you'll say something like, "We propose to meet those needs by...."

c. The Next Step. Solutions in themselves are incomplete without a follow-up strategy. This is where you say something like, "After your approval, we will initiate...."

Recently a new client turned to me in a meeting when I was presenting a marketing proposal. I had just gone through a brief summary of his needs which I had learned over the course of three meetings. Impressed, he said, "You really listened, didn't you?"

If he only knew about all the other times! I can give you many more examples when I didn't listen very well, resulting in lost business and an end to a good relationship before it even started. But that client's comments encouraged me greatly. "You really listened" is just about the highest compliment I can imagine, considering how hard it is for me to listen, just like everyone else.

What's more, with his compliment I could tell he thought I was pretty smart. Smart because I heard what he said and gave it back to him in summary form. And that's not just good for your ego, it does tremendous things for the acceptance of your proposal. Just think. If you've proven your intelligence by listening carefully, how could you then turn stupid and present an irrelevant idea? No, your proposal will have a favorable hearing because you listened carefully. It will be on target because it meets the needs you so carefully identified.

Don't hide anything.

When a salesperson appears reluctant to give me a price up front, I automatically conclude that he or she questions the value of the proposal. Perhaps you react the same way. And, as a salesperson, if you don't believe that a customer is getting his money's worth, obviously you can't expect him to believe it, either. If you hide the price, disguise it, or bury it in the proposal, it seems pretty clear that you are uncomfortable with it.

Price isn't the only thing people tend to hide in proposals. There may be a weakness in your solution that the customer will discover sooner or later. Your model pump outperforms the others, but tends to break down earlier. Or your vehicles get better mileage, but the competition has more cargo space.

You may believe that the strong points in your proposal overcome any shortcomings. And who knows? The customer may not even care about your shortcomings once they're out in the open. But if you don't bring them out your customer will get suspicious. He'll conclude that you think these flaws are fatal.

Bring it all out into the open. Prove that you understand the weakness or the trade-off, but explain why you think it is compensated for by the rest of your offer. That kind of approach shows confidence, honesty and integrity.

And don't wait until after the deal is made. The worst thing that can happen is that you get the deal and then the client finds out about your shortcomings. Remember, once a customer becomes a customer the marriage begins. Do you want to start a relationship with a lie? The resulting lack of trust creates complications in the relationship that you simply don't need.

Ask for the order.

When salespeople have trouble closing business it's almost always for one simple reason: They don't ask for the order. They're waiting for the fruit to fall off the tree, or else they try to pick the fruit while it's still green.

And if a salesperson is totally focused on getting that signed contract or purchase order, the temptation is to say something like, "All we need is for you to sign this...." If you're that salesperson, resist the temptation.

The client doesn't want to sign anything, because there's risk and pain involved in that. Sometimes great risk and pain. The only reason anyone would be willing to go through the pain is because the benefit of what you are selling more than compensates. If it's a tough sale it's because the pain and benefit nearly match. If it's an easy sale it's because the benefit clearly outweighs the pain. If you don't make the sale, well, you know.

The point is, never ask a potential customer to do what they don't want to do. Offer to give them what they want. That way, the best close is really no close at all — it's simply a smooth transition from the solution to the next step. And the best close goes something like this: "As soon as you say, we'll get to work for you."

By the way, an experienced sales person with a good antenna can normally tell when a sale is made. They look for nonverbal cues, a push back of the chair, a relaxation in demeanor. Any and all can be indications that the deal is done. When it is, it's time to stop selling and move to the close.

Know the next step in advance.

Since customers will always focus on the benefit to them, their question is "How am I going to get to that desired result as quickly as possible?" Your presentation needs to address this question. First, because it is high on your customer's mind. Second, because this is how you close the sale.

Once you believe the customer has made a mental decision to buy, stop presenting, stop selling and get to work. It doesn't matter if you're not finished or even if your best stuff is just coming up. If you know the sale is made, just say, "I could go on and on, but let's talk about how we can get this going." If you're wrong, you'll be stopped. If not, you'll be started and the honeymoon has begun.

Be gracious — win or lose.

As important as it is to keep your emotions close to your vest in the presentation, it may be even more important at the end of it. Win or lose, be gracious. Celebrate too much and you will demonstrate that getting the order has taken you totally by surprise, which doesn't say much for your confidence going in.

Much worse is demonstrating anger, bitterness or frustration at losing. Not only will you eliminate your chances for any future business, but any displays will only help destroy your reputation when this customer talks to others in the community or industry.

The best approach is to believe that any loss is only temporary, and that you will have another chance in the future. How much of a chance depends on the character you demonstrate in the face of a disappointing setback. The surprising thing is that you will get a second chance more often than you might hope for, but not if you burn your bridges.

This is true whether you have been treated fairly or not. Remember, life isn't fair and selling certainly isn't, either. You may have put your heart and soul into the sales effort only to find that the customer selected an old friend or relative who has always gotten the business. You may find you were duped into providing a proposal that was used just to get someone else to lower his price. You may find that a mean-spirited middle manager disparaged you unfairly and eliminated you from the competition. Welcome to life. The old saying "turn the other cheek" is exceedingly tough to live by and yet is very good business.

To prepare for the inevitable disappointments, practice this little exercise before hearing whether or not you have won the business. Say the next four responses out loud:

1. "Of course, we are very disappointed that you didn't select us."

2. "(The competition) is an excellent company and I'm certain they will do an excellent job for you." (Don't say this if it's clearly wrong, but try to give them the benefit of the doubt.)

3. "If for any reason, things don't work out as you expect, please give us a call. We'd be happy to serve you."

4. "If you don't mind, I would like to check back with you in (time period), just to see that everything is going well for you."

There, that wasn't so hard, was it? Okay, it was very hard, but you'll find in the long run that keeping a gracious attitude is extremely worthwhile. And once you see that, it will get easier. Not easy, just easier.

Make it hard to say no.

The bottom line of selling is this: The sale usually goes to the person to whom it is hardest to say no. If you understand this principle, you start with the question, "How can I make it as hard as possible for this prospect to say no to me?" You move toward that position throughout the entire selling process, and when you get there, you stay.

Certainly the basic elements still have to be in place, including an appropriate solution, a price that delivers value and confidence in the ability to deliver. But beyond these basics we need to remember our relationship essentials. Remember awareness, credibility, trust and chemistry?

At this stage of the selling relationship, awareness asks if the prospect clearly understands our proposed solution. Credibility checks to see whether the prospect then believes that I (or the company) can perform as promised. Does the prospect believe I would be willing to put his or her needs before my own? That's trust in action. And finally, does the prospect sense that there is a basic sharing of important values and deeper goals? Are significant interests shared? Is there a possibility of real friendship beyond the business relationship? Is there a chemistry?

You cannot manufacture awareness, credibility, trust or chemistry. If you try, you become like the overbearing car salesman who presumes to pretend the two of you have a long and abiding friendship. Or the appliance salesman who acts as if he has a deep interest in the health and well-being of your family. By following that sorry example you will lose your sales and make it very easy for prospects to tell you no.

If, on the other hand, you find a genuine place for these four essentials in your business relationships, you will also find that their effect is powerful.

"The mechanic that would perfect his work
must first sharpen his tools."
— Confucius

9

Tools:
The Next Generation

Friendship Marketing is a building block for creating effective marketing tools —
including ads, brochures, public relations programs, videos, interactive media
and more. This chapter demonstrates how starting with the customers'
motivations and interests drives effective graphic
design and communication styles.

Chapter summary:

- A brave new world.
- How to use the new tools.
  - Find out who's listening out there.
  - Find out what they want.
  - Decide what you want.
  - Bring your needs and their needs together.
- Seven checkpoints for building communication tools.
  - Materials tell a story.
  - Stories build emotion.
  - Contrast grabs attention.
  - Color molds emotions.
  - Typography sets the mood.
  - Copy and voice set the tone.
  - Information design makes it readable.
- The New Media: What makes it different.

- Linearity is different.
- We're getting information in smaller bites.
- We're making information more "scannable."
- We're creating a new hierarchy of detail.
- We're relying more on visual presentations.
- We're inventing something called "Infotainment."
- Back to Basics: Building relationships with the New Media.
  - Database systems.
  - Data capturing systems.
  - Presentation tools.
  - The Net.
    1) The Internet is uncontrolled.
    2) The Internet is global.
    3) The Internet is interactive.
    4) The Internet is user-controlled.

By now you are probably finding it hard to escape an essential theme of this book. Call it "They always come first." Or, "You first, me second." Or simply, "Sacrifice self-interest." We've seen how this theme clashes against our very nature, and we've seen how the "others first" philosophy must be in place to sell customers and build lasting business relationships. Now we're going to see how sacrificing self-interest must be the first step to creating effective marketing tools.

Some people refer to these tools as "collateral," but I hate that term. Collateral is ad agency lingo that harks back to the days when ad executives believed advertising was everything and that nothing else mattered. "Collateral" as in "collateral damage." Something alongside. Nothing really significant — not even intended.

It's a shame, really. But I think agency people may have downplayed marketing tools because they couldn't figure out how to make money with them the same way they could with the 15 percent commission for placing national ads. For them, marketing tools represented collateral revenue.

What I'm referring to here as "tools" are those varied items a company uses to communicate with its customers and prospects. Advertising and traditional public relations are also tools, but since we've already discussed them in a previous chapter we'll focus on a few other items. We could be talking about ad specialties such as mugs and caps, or perhaps brochures, data sheets, fact sheets, fax responses, direct mail, websites, interactive CD, videos, slide shows, computer-based presentations, posters, trade show booths, calendars, or .... You get the idea.

A brave new world.

It's entirely possible that someday soon marketing communicators may view the tools we now use as quaint antiques. Things like direct mail, where we rely on the post office. Or brochures, where we cut down trees, make paper, run it through a big machine and apply lots of colored ink. Even VHS video cassettes are surely destined for a place in the marketing museums, even though today advanced marketers are using them to distribute promotional messages to far-flung audiences.

Today a new generation of marketing tools is almost certain to revolutionize how people communicate with one another. That, in turn, will change the way relationships are built and how business is done. And those same tools, though relying on the most advanced technology of our day, also provide the brightest potential for businesses to focus on building key relationships.

You could almost call them "Friendship Marketing" tools, although I hesitate to name them because new ones are emerging so quickly. Even as you read this, new spins are being put on old tools. So as soon as I name them they may be outdated; I know I'll have to rewrite this section soon. Having said that, however, I'll take the risk and name a few tools that fit the "Friendship Marketing" category right now:

- Database systems, including advanced contact management software

- Data collection devices that enable immediate capture of valuable customer information such as barcode systems and kiosks.

- Presentation creation tools that enable quick customization:

- Interactive media including CD-ROMs.

- And probably most significant of all, the Internet and its communication form known as the World Wide Web.

You may have noticed the pattern. Yes, these new tools all boil down to one word: computers. When some genius figured out how to make silicon calculate 0s and 1s, he probably couldn't have imagined how they were going to turn the world upside down.

Now we're seeing that the computer has ushered in the most dramatic changes in society since the Industrial Revolution. The computer, not even a word in dictionaries a short generation ago, has become so central in the lives of every person on the globe that our "modern" era is said to have begun with it.

For our purposes, the computer and all its communication manifestations have become the most powerful tools in the hands of marketers since the words, "How can I help you?" were first spoken. But unless we understand how to use the computer to build real relationships between real people, this tool can turn against us as the greatest enemy of relationship building.

Look at how computer technology has been used in national marketing efforts, and you see how few people really understand its power to build relationships. Far more people use the computer as a shortcut, or even a replacement to relationship building. They would be better off throwing all their computers out the window, along with all the expensive software, and get out of the office to start shaking hands.

How to use the new tools.

Of course there is a better way. But before we explore how the "New Tools" (I mean, computer) can be used to help build key relationships, let's take a step backwards. Let's rediscover how to effectively use all tools, new or old. When we're designing and creating effective marketing tools, the main thing is an old-fashioned concept: "Put the customer first." (I use the word "customer." Feel free to substitute "reader," "viewer," "audience," "prospect" or whatever term is appropriate to you.)

Find out who's listening out there.

Amazing, when you think about the implications. Yet it is painfully obvious that far too many brochures, direct mail pieces, videos and sale presentations are prepared with no clear audience in mind. Can you imagine making a sales call over the phone and saying, "Hello everyone?"

We may design a mailing piece that will go to 5,000 names. That's fine. We may not know exactly who the readers are, but we must remember that the mailer will be read one at a time, by individual people with distinct interests and styles.

If you understand this challenge you see that mass promotion is frequently wasted. Even when marketers have done their homework and they've focused their mailing list (or their key contact list), they often treat all their readers in the same way. They create a brochure, video or data sheet as if the audience were made up of 100 percent clones.

Big mistake. There is literally no way to address every need of a very diverse and unknown group. If "everyone" is the reader, then "no one" will be the real reader, just as surely as if everyone is responsible, then no one is responsible. Hence the basic idea of focusing on the right few.

Why spend a lot of money trying to reach a lot of people who don't really matter to you — and not even do a good job of that? Why not focus the same dollars on finding the right few whose needs you are reasonably assured you can meet?

One of the best ways to find those few is through creative focus. And one of the most powerful tools that effective creative people have to design and write strong promotional messages is the idea of talking to one person. In other words, if you want to design a powerful mailer or sales brochure, start with a single person. Make it someone you know, someone you can picture. Imagine that person sitting across the coffee table from you. What would you say? How would you approach the subject? How would you make certain you had the person's interest and attention?

If you start with a clear concept of who that reader or customer is, your marketing piece will have far more power and impact. Throw out the "everyone" and start talking to "someone." One person whose interests and concerns and personality you can grasp and picture.

Try this. Let's say you are creating a new capabilities brochure for your company. The first step is to throw out all your old ideas about how to create a capabilities brochure. Don't start thinking about where your logo is going, or the color of the paper, or how many pictures of your new office you want to include. Start by thinking about one customer. Maybe it's a very good customer and a good friend. Maybe it's someone you would love to have as a very good customer. Got that person in mind? Not yet? Fine, I'll wait.

Find out what they want.

Now that you have someone in mind, it's easy to go to the next step. Say you want to sell an idea to someone you don't know very well. In fact, you're trying to sell Daddy Warbucks on investing in your new Internet publishing company. About all you know at the start is that this person likes to invest in the right kind of business projects.

You meet in a busy restaurant, a place that turns out to be frequented by people fishing for Mr. Warbucks' money. No sooner are you seated than three people come up to him in turn and say, "Mr. Warbucks, I have something that you will really find interesting." One says, "Mr. Warbucks, I'll let you in on the ground floor of an investment that will make you zillions."

It becomes pretty clear that you have a lot of competition for Mr. Warbucks' attention, just like your brochure will have when your customer or prospect comes across it.

What to do? You already know that Mr. Warbucks makes investments and you know he has plenty of opportunity. You need to find out what he considers a good investment and how he decides what kind of investments to make. So you start asking questions: What are your investment criteria? Fast return? Big return? Promising new technologies or safe, certain low-risk types? Do you invest more in ideas or people? Is it important for you to have a role in what you invest in?

Those are just a few of your queries. Once you learn some of the answers you can either make your pitch or pick up the check and save Mr. Warbucks some time so he can go on to things that interest him more.

But that's selling, you say. And that was covered in the last chapter.

Exactly the point. Your brochure, video or trade show booth has to perform; it has to sell. The only difference is that with a brochure you don't have the advantage of being able to ask questions as you make your presentation. (Hint: Here's why the "New Tools" are so exciting. We'll discuss them soon.)

If you can't ask questions, you have do your research first. If you haven't done it, you can't do your brochure. It's like pitching Mr. Warbucks before you have any idea of his interests. Once you've determined his particular interests, you proceed. And of course you are going to start out with what interests him the most.

As you do, keep two challenges in mind. First, remember that Mr. Warbucks is probably more complicated than you might think. Chances are it isn't one simple thing but a combination of factors that will determine his interest in making any investment. Chances are he will have twenty needs, not just one, which multiplies the challenge.

You can deal with the ambiguity of Mr. Warbucks and his needs. But remember that we're not talking about personal selling, and that's our second challenge. We're talking about selling through something like a video or a brochure.

We're also not preparing this sales pitch for just one person, we're making 5,000 copies for at least that many prospects. Our second challenge reads like a math class story problem: How can you address 100,000 needs in one opening sentence, using a single headline? Answer: You can't. Simple as that. Please don't try.

Trying to address too many needs at one time is the primary killer of otherwise good sales material. First we prioritize our audience. Then we prioritize their needs. And because there are so many potential investors out there, you can afford to choose the ones that fit the best, the ones most likely to match. Generally it's most productive to choose them as a group sharing some significant point of interest.

Perhaps you decide the key for your prospects is their willingness to take a chance on an exciting new application of technology. That defines them as a group. Other investors may be interested for other reasons, but if you try to accommodate all those reasons, you'll miss the mark. Aiming for everyone leaves you with no one.

So you've prioritized the audience, and in the process probably cut your press run from 5,000 to 1,000. Smart move, but you still have the issue of Mr. Warbucks' mixed priorities. Of course, he's not terribly unique; all of us are a hodgepodge of needs and desires. Ultimately, though, we can focus on what is really important.

Maybe Mr. Warbucks doesn't really know what's ultimately important to him because no one has actually asked him before. But you have, because you're smart and a good listener and you know how to ask the right questions. In your conversation in that busy restaurant, you picked up on a brief interchange between Mr. Warbucks and one of the many people who interrupted him. You concluded that Mr. Warbucks considered it very important to show that he was not only keeping up with things but ahead of the game. He obviously valued being able to tell his friends and associates how he had seen something coming that they hadn't.

With that assumption in mind, you asked him to tell you about his recent investments and you saw that they fit a pattern. He used phrases like, "ahead of the game" and "being the first." Aha. You saw what was really important to him: being perceived by others as visionary.

Your conversation turns. "Mr. Warbucks," you say boldly, "I perceive that you are somewhat of a visionary in your investing. If that's true, I have something that I think will be of considerable interest to you." Your pitch has begun. And your brochure or video message starts to take shape. Its core message? What else: "Ahead of the Game."

Decide what you want.

At this point most people start creating their tools. And I say if they start with a clear purpose in mind they are light years ahead of those who start with the purpose of simply putting out a brochure or creating a company video. Toolmaking is really not the first step.

For one thing, thinking through the question of what your customers really want may lead you to decide that doing a brochure is actually a bad idea. The client might be better off spending money on trade shows, producing a catalog or sending personal letters. Of course it takes listening and work to make that determination.

Once you determine what is really important to your "right few," once you get a fix on their primary interest point, it's important to be very clear about the objectives of the tool you are creating. Try asking these eight questions:

1. Do you want to sell your product or service directly from this tool?

2. Do you want the tool to help identify prospects, those "right few?"

3. Do you want to introduce your company in a low-key, non-intimidating way?

4. Do you want to increase awareness of the range of services you offer to people who may only know part of what you do?

5. Do you want to increase your credibility with people who may only know you a little now?

6. Do you want to introduce a new product or service to existing customers?

7. Do you want to change how your customers think of you?

8. Do you want to help customers more clearly understand how you differ from your main competitor?

If you don't have a clear purpose in mind, don't start creating your tool. Not yet. If you're working with an agency or designer or writer, don't ask them to do anything for you until you can answer the eight previous questions. But don't worry, they're summed up in two basic questions that any good communications professional should ask: Who is the audience and what do you want to accomplish?

If you don't have a purpose, take a blank piece of paper and write down: "After reading this brochure (or viewing this video...) my customer (prospect, audience, friend ...) will _____." Then you fill in the blank. Be reasonable. Be realistic. But be crystal clear.

Now it makes more sense, if you follow these steps. You have a purpose in mind and your customer has a purpose in mind. Those two have to come together. But to bring them together you have to start with the other person. It's like my sister says (jokingly) after talking about herself for awhile, "But enough about me, let's talk about you. Tell me, what do you think about me?"

Admittedly, it's very hard to subordinate our own purposes, interests and needs. That's why we're in business in the first place, to take care of our needs and those of our family. But we won't take care of our needs if we don't take care of others. Start there. The rest will follow.

Bring your needs and their needs together.

The decisions you make to reconcile your needs with the needs of others will determine your marketing tool and its effectiveness. One follows the other. And here are a few of the questions that will be answered as you focus on the customer.

1. Which tool should I use? (letter, brochure, video, interactive presentation ...)

2. What kind of format is best? (brochure size, video length, number of pages to the letter ...)

3. How about approach? (documentary style, straight facts, dependent on visuals ...)

4. Which style is most appropriate? (corporate, designerly, elegant, cutting edge ...)

5. And what about content? (level of detail, information design, nature of information ...)

Most people make these decisions based mainly on personal preference, not on what's best for the client. Big mistake. The writer decides what kind of writing style he or she likes. The designer decides what kind of graphic style he or she likes. And the client says he or she likes this or that simply on their personal tastes. Who gives a rat's rump about anyone's personal tastes? The only thing that matters is whether your tool gives your readers what they want and whether it fulfills the purpose. That's it. Every discussion should be centered around those two guidelines. Anything else is irrelevant.

If anyone in the process says, "I don't like the size of this image as it relates to this headline," their objection should be followed with the reason why the format detracts from what the reader wants or how it could be changed to more adequately meet the intended purpose of the piece. If the critic can't give a reason, then frankly the objection is meaningless.

And of course, the discussions get even more interesting when several strong-minded people stake a claim on the final piece. The size of a budget is directly related to the size of egos in the management group involved with the project. The more egos, the bigger the budget. The bigger the egos the bigger the budget. Lots of big egos, well, you get the picture.

It may be simpler to bring a reader's wants and your needs together if we think about all communication as fulfilling one of three essential purposes:

1. Information

2. Entertainment

3. Inspiration

I didn't list selling as an essential purpose here because we're taking the customer's perspective. Think about it, and you'll realize that you have probably never picked up a brochure or watched a TV commercial because you were eager for someone to sell you something. You may want information to help you make a decision. You may want to learn about something you didn't know existed. But I can't think of too many times when I watched or listened to a promotional message because I wanted someone to sell me. I wanted information, entertainment or inspiration.

Thinking about your readers and their desires or needs in those terms will help you decide how to structure your sales tool. As you decide, answer two questions: Is the information you have valuable to them? Will it help them meet their goals? If you can answer "yes" to both questions, then use a straightforward approach to present your information. The quicker and easier you make it for your audience to get what they want, the happier they will be. If information is not the issue, however, you may need to look at entertainment.

Consider your favorite brand of soda, and how much information you need about that brand. It may have a certain amount of sweetener or a particular mix of ingredients. The manufacturer may keep it in warehouses only a few days so that it's fresh when you get it. But generally you don't need to know all those specifics to choose and drink your soda. So if soda advertisers are going to get us to pay attention to their brand, they're going to have to entertain us. They're going to have to capture our interest through things that on the surface have little or nothing to do with the product, like children of the world singing on a mountain top to sell us Coke. Or cute polar bears sliding down a hill on a sled. These kinds of messages entertain us and help sell products.

In a selling message, however, entertainment can never be its own purpose. In other words, it must do something more, by helping differentiate the product or build awareness. It must serve the purpose of selling the product.

Unfortunately, many creative marketers forget this simple requirement. They seem to think that entertaining is enough. For example, characters in an ad campaign must personify your brand or product, like the highly successful Energizer bunny or George Whipple, the shopkeeper who spent 21 years convincing his shoppers not to squeeze the Charmin.

Entertainment works. The bunny has become one of America's best-loved TV icons while drumming up market share for his Energizer batteries; the Whipple character helped squeeze out the competition while Charmin become the country's top tissue. And many people remember the movie that propelled Reese's candy sales through the roof: *ET*.

Creativity blurs the line between entertainment and selling, and that's as it should be. Once you have clearly identified what the reader wants and what you want, then the real task is to blend the two. It's the creative process. It is bringing order out of chaos. It is bringing something totally new into the world. To me, getting involved in the creative process is just about the most exciting thing anyone can do in life.

Seven checkpoints for building communication tools.

Your marketing tool begins to take shape on the foundation of clearly identified purposes. Now you can ask the question that finally makes sense. Instead of just relying on personal preference, is your tool the very best way to accomplish the purpose? Let's look at seven checkpoints, seven ways to see whether your tool measures up. Each factor will have to stand up to the standard of giving the reader or viewer what he or she really wants.

Materials tell a story.

Every college journalism student knows the famous quote from Marshall McLuhan: The medium is the message. Decades after he said that, it's still true. The way you say something becomes more important than what you say. Form and materials tend to communicate more than the message.

For example, if you rely on personal letters rather than expensive brochures, that says one thing. If you print your brochure on rough recycled paper containing little wood chips, that sends an environmentally-oriented message. If your sales video goes to the client with a handwritten label and your company name is spelled wrong, that sends a message as well. Every element of your marketing material contributes to or detracts from your purpose, just as in a personal sales call.

Stories build emotion.

There should be a whole book on the power of story in marketing. Humans love stories, and I'm certain storytelling is our oldest form of education and entertainment. Imagine Og and Glog in the cave grunting out with gestures exactly where they found the mastodon and how they climbed up on its back before dispatching the beast.

We love stories about people. In a review of the top news stories of the decade, the story of the dramatic rescue of a small girl who fell down a well in Texas was near the top. C'mon. Thousands of people were killed in tragic wars and plagues. Earthquakes and floods devastated millions of families. Political changes around the world rocked millions of lives. And the most memorable story is about a little girl being pulled from a well? If that isn't a testament to the power of story, I don't know what is.

People are endlessly fascinating. Character is the most gripping element of movies, drama, novels and advertising. Take a look at the captivating stories of Sharon and Tony, television advertising neighbors who helped perk up sales of Taster's Choice coffee through their intriguing, half-finished relationship that was serialized over a series of TV ads starting in the early '90s. Yet for all their success, using character to sell is a frequently overlooked technique.

Look at how you can deliver your sales message through story. Customer stories are one way. Think of a real employee who can epitomize what service means in your company. Or create a character to represent your product or service. Any way you present the stories, people are endlessly fascinated by watching real or imaginary people.

And we've always been this way. A couple of mothers in Northern California have sold hundreds of thousands of videotapes to families and daycare centers. Young kids drop what they're doing and gather around the VCR to stare, transfixed at the images of ... babies. Just babies, for nearly a full half-hour. They stare, and the audience stares back.

Okay, so adults are different. But are we? Add a little plot, overlay a bit of dialogue. Yet the concept remains. We stare at the faces of the people, wondering if they're not just a bit like us.

Celebrity ads are more than just borrowing someone's success. The good ones borrow the character, and such a technique often works quite well, indeed. The risk is that the person's character will turn out to reflect poorly on the company. Tarnished personal reputations of some superstars have caused major headaches for companies like Pepsi. But sometimes the bad boy character is used to help clearly differentiate the product, especially if it's aimed toward young people.

As we further blur the line between information and entertainment, story will become increasingly important. Story is inherently educational. It can also convey information more powerfully than nearly anything else. As such it may be the one way to combine all three purposes of information, education and inspiration.

Contrast grabs attention.

"White space is my friend" is a mantra we often repeat in our graphics department when trying to argue a design issue with a client. Clients tend to dislike white space. It seems an expensive luxury. But the issue is not that designers love white space. The issue is contrast.

Take a newspaper with nothing but copy or text. We call it a gray page. Now, open up a little section in the middle and put nothing in it. Just empty space, white space. What happens? Your eyes go there. Automatically. You almost can't stop it.

Theatrical artists know this technique well. Most stages have thick black curtains called "blacks." Put a whole row of actors on the stage with the blacks stretched across the stage behind them. If the house lights are on or lights flood the stage, the audience's eyes wander from one person to the other without direction. Now, turn all the lights off except a little spot light focused on the face of a single actor. The contrast between black and white forces your eye to the point of contrast. You can't help it. Put a black dot on a clean white sheet and the effect is the same.

Contrast is the main technique designers use to control the flow of the eye across the page or across the screen. Take away the designer's opportunity to use contrast and you take away her main design tool. (As in, "There's too much white space — I'm paying for that space, you know.") Do that, and you would be asking her to do her job with one hand tied behind her back. I'll tell you it drives designers nuts and it should. Make sure white space is your friend, too.

Color molds emotions.

Color is primarily a tool of contrast, not a separate tool in itself. There are many in design who would argue, and there have been endless studies on the power and meaning of color. I won't dispute those. Red does have a different emotional impact than blue or green. But its real impact is when seen in contrast to other colors. When used in the right context, color becomes a powerful tool to communicate information, grab attention, and inspire deep emotional responses.

Clients will often ask things like, "What color should my logo be?" as if there were a universal right or wrong color. Or if you put a yellow background on a certain brochure you hear the objection that the client doesn't like yellow. Again, let me say it as clearly as possible: Personal preferences mean nothing. Your favorite color means nothing. There is really only one question to ask when you are trying to justify choosing one color over another: How does this help accomplish my purpose? And since my purpose is helping my customer or reader accomplish their purpose, that becomes the question.

Related questions help you answer the primary question. How does choosing the color yellow (in this example) help accomplish the client's goals? Does it draw attention to itself? Does it distract? Does it create the right emotional atmosphere? All those are good questions to which there are no 100 percent objective, right answers.

Hindsight will give you some good clues, but none of us possess hindsight before the fact. Better than that, the customers or readers have the right answers. When in doubt, ask them. At the very least, agree that they are the ones who matter.

Typography sets the mood.

Type is another important tool of the designer, similar to color. And again, there are no "right" or "wrong" typestyles, except as they relate to audience perception and contribute to customer goals.

Of course, there is no question that some kinds of typestyles are easier to read than others. Some typestyles become invisible by blending into our background perception and not drawing attention to themselves. They should be chosen for the vast majority of written marketing material, and include the basic Roman serif fonts such as Palatino (used in this book), as well as the classic sans serif fonts such as Helvetica and Univers.

But beware: Fonts often carry their own meaning and in some cases become part of the message. Don't forget McLuhan. Typestyle in headlines is very important in conveying the meaning you want to communicate. And sometimes you want the type to actually become intrusive and draw attention to itself. Your choice of typestyle will depend on one question, just as your choice of color depended on one question: Does the typestyle help give the reader what he or she wants, and help to achieve the business purpose?

Copy and voice set the tone.

There is much that can be said about copy in marketing material. Copy is a little like the Army, while visuals and headlines serve as the Air Force. Strategic bombing and aerial supremacy (visuals and headlines) can accomplish much, but ultimately the war is won on the ground. That's where the copy comes in.

There's a simple rule of thumb for knowing how much copy is needed. Only as much as it takes to get the job done. No more. So if the purpose is to make a complex sale through the marketing material alone (as in classic direct marketing ads or direct mail) the copy is probably going to be somewhat long and very complete. If it is only to build awareness and generate interest, the copy is probably going to be short. Either way, it's important to predetermine your voice.

What I'm calling "voice" may very well be the most important decision you make about copy. When the reader reads the words, think of what style or personality should be conveyed. You can choose a voice that is warm, friendly and personal. Elegant and literary. Technical and informative. You can reach the heart or the head, or both.

If you're not sure of the tone, read the words aloud. Ask others if it sounds like a lecturer, a preacher or a friend. The ways in which words are strung together and the specific words that are chosen are extremely important in conveying the message. And like color or other design elements, voice is often a matter of discussion and controversy between client and writer. Unlike color and typestyle, however, the issues may not be clearly understood. So the client may say, "I don't like the way this sounds."

Again, the client's personal preferences ultimately matter very little. The questions remain the same. Is the language used appropriate for the reader? Will the right impression be created? Does it contribute to the purpose?

If the language doesn't contribute to the purpose, by all means edit. Change the copy. Start over. Be merciless. Writers frequently make the mistake of writing in a voice inappropriate for the reader or the client. The voice needs to be consistent with how the reader understands the company. Somehow, you don't expect a Mercedes ad to start with, "Howdy, folks. How y'all do'n? Your friend Cal here to talk about a super duper car." The voice is quite wrong. Make sure it's right.

Information design makes it readable.

Information design is a relatively new term for a relatively new process that helps us sift through the sea of information flooding our lives each day. We all know how overwhelming the flood can become. Richard Saul Wurman, a leading expert on information design, calls our condition "information anxiety" in his book by the same name. Information design seeks to treat this anxiety and transform content into meaning by understanding how people take in data in this over-mediated world.

Actually, most of the marketing techniques we have been talking about have come about because of our intense environment. Often it takes a marketing communications professional to cut through the clutter.

In the same way, everything we have been talking about relates to information design, now more than ever. While traditional media are restricted by a history of "linear" communication, the interactive new media were born for a world overwhelmed by data. And today's communication professional needs to understand principles of information design, whether dealing with traditional or new media. That's what the next section is all about.

The New Media: What makes it different.

There really is a big difference. New media are not just the electronic offspring of the old media. I hesitate to use the word revolutionary, but it fits. New media are nonlinear, giving the audience new control.

Linearity is different.

Here's what I mean. Broadcast television is linear. Books and most written material are linear. Videos are very linear. You have a beginning, a middle and an end.

You cannot easily meander, and it is either difficult or impossible to view linear media backwards.

Television, another linear medium, presents us with a steady stream of light and sound. When the station or network decides you are finished with one thing, they give you something else. About six minutes of programming, then commercial messages interspersed with little previews of what's coming ahead so you don't wander off.

When there was one channel, television was exceptionally linear. The only control the audience had was to turn it on or off, or leave the room. With a few more channels, TV became slightly less linear because now you could get up and change the channel. Generally it was too far to the set, though, so it was easier to sit and watch whatever was on.

Then came the remote, which gave us even more freedom. The programs were still linear, but zapping became a phenomenon and a worry for both advertisers and Nielsen. Soon the VCR took away even more "linearity." Now my Dad can tape "Wheel of Fortune" and watch it whenever he darn well pleases, not when a network programmer decides. He can even avoid commercials by fast forwarding or with equipment that will eliminate them entirely.

Books, brochures and newspapers tended to be very linear in the past. You read the first paragraph, the second, and so on. Newspapers were the least linear because headlines screamed for attention, while the reader could scan and decide which story to go to first or last. But once into the story, the reader lost control. The information was very linear.

One notable departure came when *USA Today* was launched in September of 1982. The paper caused a stir because it introduced nonlinear concepts into news articles; it also increased reader control of the entire paper. And because of the paper's visual approach, some accused the publisher of making newspapers just like TV. Some called it the "MacDonaldization" of news. Many critics decried it as the end of literacy. And then slowly most newspapers copied it.

Just like books, brochures and sales materials have tended to be very linear. Writers and designers seem to think that with so much information to present, we should just start at the beginning and run it through to the end. Trouble is, the beginning and end depend on what is logical to the writer and designer. And the information becomes the dictator, the controlling point.

In reality readers or viewers always want to control. With the popularity of interactive media, they're telling us to "give us what we want, give it to us now, make it quick, and then let us decide how much further we want to go with this." Are we listening?

National Geographic magazine provides a classic example of semi-linear information design. Almost all articles have two information tracks; one primarily visual and the other primarily verbal, or written. Most of the information in a story can be gleaned from either track. In other words, you don't need to look at the pictures to gain most of the information. At the same time, the photos with their brief captions also contain most of the information, too. The reader can choose how he or she wants to learn. For more detailed study, they usually choose both tracks.

Generally, the more linear the communication the more the information is controlled by the speaker or sender of the message. The more nonlinear, the more it is controlled by the receiver of the message. Since most of us want more control, most of us prefer nonlinear — as long as the convenience is equal. And the convenience factor has given traditional formats (newspapers, brochures, broadcast TV, radio, etc.) their advantage up to now. But as the new media increase in convenience, there is little doubt the advantage of viewer control will be decisive.

This kind of shift means that marketers must take the new media seriously. It also means they do well to adapt traditional media techniques and replicate the advantages of reader control as much as possible. That's because a brochure or newspaper is not inherently linear — it's just the information design style that has become the convention. And conventions are changing, becoming less linear. Here are a few more ways information design is changing.

We're getting information in smaller bites.

Let's take two pages, both containing the same information and virtually the same number of words. In one version lay out the script so one word follows another with only the traditional paragraph breaks in between. In the other, break it up into small sections, each with its own defining space and each with its own small headline. Then ask people which page they would prefer reading.

You already know the answer. And the reason why most would prefer the more segmented version is simple. When we see the information as a series of self-contained units, we feel less of a commitment to read the whole thing.

But we face a gray page (unbroken text) reluctantly unless we are eager for the information. If we don't know the content or we're unsure how it applies to us, we much prefer the least challenging version. Break up the information for more inviting reading.

We're making information more "scannable."

Scannable information invites the reader to do a quick skim for an overall perspective. Then it allows readers to choose where they want to dive in.

The page should be like a menu. Here are your choices. Start with dessert if you want, then go to the appetizer. Begin where you want, end where you want. If there is reason to start at a particular point, the scannable tool will provide the reason without forcing the reader to choose.

You can increase scanability in a brochure by listing the contents in a sidebar at the beginning or by providing a headline on every section or paragraph. Before asking the reader to commit to the information, the headline gives a brief preview of the information in that paragraph. (If you look closely, you may notice some of these suggested techniques at work in this book. Practice what you preach, you know.)

We're creating a new hierarchy of detail.

Some people want lots of detail, some none, and some just a little. You can reach them all by offering many choices and not forcing a choice.

Say you have a sales brochure about a new insurance product. Some just want the bare minimum: "What's in it for me and make it snappy." Then they'll decide if they want to take the next step. Others want to have a few questions answered before they decide to go on. And a few need every little detail nailed down.

It's difficult to please all three kinds of people, but it is possible. Your brochure design and layout will be determined by how you decide to accommodate the different sets of desires and expectations.

We're relying more on visual presentations.

Today it's a common idea that we have become a visual society. And it's true we have come to rely on photos and images to a greater degree than ever, perhaps more than since the time of the Egyptians.

Good news, or bad? Many complain that the visual trend threatens everything from our ability to think clearly to Western Civilization as we know it. They have pleaded for a return to a more verbal and literary means of communication. (See the book *Amusing Ourselves to Death* by Neil Postman.)

I don't share those views, and I believe the health of the book publishing and magazine industries bears me out. Besides, I think we can look to a longstanding history of thinking in pictures. Let's not forget that our first written languages were essentially pictograms or hieroglyphics, visual symbols for meaning. Many languages today, particularly the Japanese Kanji and Chinese, provide evidence of the visual nature of verbal language.

Maybe it was television that turned us from words to pictures. But it's not just TV. In our global society, images are a language that are beginning to transcend cultures as well as words. A sad expression on a young child communicates across cultural boundaries. A joyous dance goes beyond ethnic differences. One company which does increasing business around the globe is creating a corporate book using just photos. The story can be told that way. No words needed. The language is universal.

Of course, major national magazines developed photojournalism into an art in the 1940s, '50s and '60s. And most people understood the impact photos would have on our society decades ago. But I'll mention them again — *USA Today* rediscovered the power not only of photo images in communicating, but also of pictograms. They showed how little graphics and charts could communicate a vast amount of real information in a single visual.

Today the revived pictograms have been adopted by magazines such as *Time* and *Newsweek*. Marketing materials are using pictograms more and more, too. And it was inevitable that the electronic media adopted graphics as their own. Apple Computer remade the word "icon."

Once upon a time an icon was a religious image that conveyed meaning, a symbol of deep spiritual truth that went far beyond the person or story depicted. Now icon is a computer term, a very small visual representation of a file or even an entire complex program. Similarly, logo which meant "word" or "idea," has been transformed into a visual shorthand that can represent a vast campaign, a product or a whole conglomerate.

We're inventing something called "Infotainment."

Not too long ago the head of the company that spends more money on advertising than anyone in the world shocked the advertising community by saying that advertising was dead.

He meant that all the rules are changing, and he was right. For years advertisers have relied on a captive audience dependent on a linear flow of images, particularly on TV. Viewers have been forced to see the commercials mainly because they want to see the programs. But zapping has changed all that; when 500 channels of video options arrive the rules will change even more. (Actually, 500 channels is already a joke. With the Internet, there is now a capacity for virtually millions of channels).

That executive knew the only way you will choose to watch commercials is if they are entertaining, or informational or inspirational on their own. In other words, only if they become program content. And if commercials become program content, it's unclear if they are still commercials. What is very clear is that the line has been crossed. The once-clear separation between programming and commercial messages is crumbling. Old-fashioned advertising is breathing its last, or at the very least it's going through drastic changes.

The change in commercials is especially evident when you look at children. Kids are barraged by a constant stream of high impact images. When they take a break from their favorite movies or TV programs to play a video game, you can be sure they're not going to sit still through some pedantic recitation of historical dates and facts. No, if they're going to learn about the battle of Agincourt, they'll have to grab their joysticks and fight with the British longbowmen or the French chivalry. If they're going to discover endangered species they're going to expect a CD with full-color video clips and stereo sound.

They call it "edutainment" and of course the purists are crying, "It's the end of the world." The reality is, this is the way kids learn and interact with their world. And the dominance of this new hands-on style is inevitable, at least until the pendulum swings back to British-style classical education.

Marketers have the same problem as educators. A highly motivated prospect wanting to know the specs on your latest laser printer will willingly wade through a certain amount of technical data. But to get someone's attention long enough to communicate product benefits or differentiation, you're going to have to entertain. Future-oriented marketers are finding all kinds of creative ways to get their vital information through entertainment.

Back to Basics: Building relationships with the New Media.

There's something interesting going on in these high-tech, high-touch days. We are right now in the process of undoing the great industrial revolution. We are turning back time to the days of the street-side merchant of the Middle Ages.

And it's made possible through today's technology, specifically the new communication media. But before we look at what's happening today, let's quickly return to the 1920s.

Henry Ford had a marvelous idea. He could serve the customer better, providing a better vehicle for less money, through mass production. In what would become a model for the world, he organized his automobile plant through specialization, then produced a mass quantity of cars involving very limited choices. (I believe it was Mr. Ford who said, "Have it any color you want as long as it is black.")

As a product of the Industrial Revolution, we've been operating that way ever since. Ford's assembly line is the model for competing in a highly competitive market by reducing costs and gaining economies of scale. Just look at fast food giants like McDonald's.

Going back even farther, it's obvious that the medieval cobbler wasn't so efficient. In the morning he'd open his shutters and drop his shelf out onto the street to display his wares. When a customer came by, he would talk, measure, discuss materials and construction, haggle out prices and terms, and take the order. Then he'd go to work and when the shoes were done the customer came by to see if they fit.

Ford would say that you couldn't build cars like that. But my point is that we've come full circle, back to the medieval model, only with a significant twist. In his brilliant book *Relationship Marketing*, Regis McKenna wrote that in the future (the very near future, it turns out) the market will return to a decidedly more personal scale.

So when you're ready to get a car you go shopping on your computer. Not for the car, but for all the latest systems, techniques, technologies and colors that are being offered by the companies. When you select your supplier, you tell him what kind of wheels, what kind of seats, what kind of instrumentation, what kind of engine. Push "send" and in a few weeks your car is delivered. McKenna calls this the "productization of service and servicization of products." The differences between manufacturing and service are disappearing as custom manufacturing gains ground.

Though it may not seem like it at first, this change has everything to do with relationship building. And the change has only been made possible because of one tool: the computer. Today's computers have made it possible for companies of all sizes to get to know their customers extremely well and to respond to them on a much more personal basis.

Consider mass mailings before the computer. You remember how they were all mailed to someone named "Occupant," or perhaps printed metal cards were used to print an individual mailing label on the outside of the mailer.

After the computer everything changed. Today mailings aren't just personally addressed. Now my *Time* magazine prints my name in the middle of the magazine and tells me how each of my elected officials in Washington voted on the issues discussed in the magazine.

But even that kind of personalization relies on traditional linear form. Subscribe to the interactive magazine called *Pathfinder* and the opportunities for customized information become staggering. I can control exactly which votes I want checked on and reported in the publication. That personalized letter will also mention items of specific interest to me captured in a wide variety of ways.

Perhaps knowing that a computer is doing the personalization detracts from the advantage of personalization. The computer may figure out that I have a new baby because I bought diapers and formula at the grocery store and that data was captured by the barcode scanner at the cash register. It may then address and send me a letter telling me about a great buy on diapers, but that's hardly personal, is it?

I'll agree, it would be better to meet Mr. Eerkes, the old grocer, and have him invite me to come into his little store for the special. But just because the computer sent the letter doesn't diminish my interest in getting a good deal on diapers. Fact is, the new system meets my specific needs. It's personalized, it's useful and it works.

And that's just one example. Let's look at a few of the other New Media tools and see how they can help in this process of relationship building.

Database systems.

To understand database systems better, just think of them as fancy filing cabinets filled with all kinds of details. Apply these details to your key customers. If you're in real estate sales you may want to capture details like the names of your good customer's kids and when they graduate from high school. You collect that information not just to send a congratulations card, but because you know empty nesters often make a change in real estate.

Or, if you're a national marketer of kitty litter you may want to put into your database the names of people who are new buyers of cat food, if there was such data. And if you were selling a new computer software program you'd be very interested in the names of people who just bought a home computer. The possibilities are endless, and they all revolve around the creative use of database systems.

Data capturing systems.

By now one of the things that should be obvious is the ultimate importance of getting information from customers and prospects. Earlier we called this listening and market research, and now we're calling it data capture. That's because automated systems are being created all the time to help marketers get better market information. This information will help focus our marketing efforts and help prevent us from wasting time and money.

With properly used data capture, I shouldn't have to mail to 20,000 homes in the countryside, hoping someone has a pet ferret because I want to sell new ferret sweaters. (That is, sweaters made for ferrets, not from ferrets.) It's much more efficient to find out who has the ferrets and mail just to those 250 homes. In theory, that data can be captured from scanner data at major pet retailers.

In reality, personal information is being captured at such an amazing rate that it's a frightening thing for a lot of people. The good news for those who are frightened is that very few people seem to know this data exists, how to get it or how to use it most effectively. Still, ever more sophisticated data collection tools are being created every day and marketers are starting to learn to use this vast sea of data. With this information, we can pinpoint potential customers, the "right few" who will make a difference for our business.

Presentation tools.

In 1986 a computer layout program called PageMaker revolutionized the graphic design and the marketing communication business. Overnight, this program did more for the graphic industry than nearly any other tool had done since Gutenberg. With it, artists could throw away their scissors and glue, producing complex designs and ads on the computer screen before they were ever printed. Soon there were dozens of similar products, and an entire desktop design industry was spawned.

Ah, but you should have heard it. In the beginning, there were howls and doomsday predictions from those who thought PageMaker and its clones would spell the end of good graphic design. But of course just the opposite proved true.

Desktop publishing tools not only created more freedom, they put great power in the hands of many more people. And today there are probably five times more people employed in graphic design than there were then. Costs have fallen while opportunities have increased as we have all become more dependent on the effective presentation and customization of information. That's been positive.

Today desktop video, interactive and presentation tools are doing the same thing for communication that PageMaker did for graphics. Everyone has access to better and more powerful tools. We have more options. Opportunities are opening up.

A software company created a slick little inventory management system. They knew it would work for auto parts stores, hardware stores, even pharmacies. But their sales literature wasn't working because their spec sheets made no distinction between potential users. Small retailers, the potential customers, just couldn't visualize how the program could work specifically for them.

It was only after the software company created a specific sheet for hardware stores and a specific one for pharmacies that they started to capture some interest. With a simple layout program they created design templates that could be customized for individual markets — even individual customers. On a tight budget, they produced attractive full-color brochures in small quantities using a color laser printer. It was all made possible because of the new technologies.

The list of new possibilities created by new technologies goes on and on, despite the question of "genuine" personalization. If you're still wondering, ask yourself which would work better — a fifteen-minute slide show meant for a wide variety of customers, or one that specifically addressed the needs of your company? I don't know about you, but I would be more impressed knowing that an entire computer-based presentation was prepared just for my eyes.

Today's presentation tools make that kind of customization easy and cost effective. The greater the flexibility built into these communication tools, the more you can use them to address specific customer interests. This is what opportunity is all about.

The Net.

The Internet, our growing worldwide web of computer link-ups, caught the public's attention in the mid-1990s. Many people discovered a new world full of friendships, the same kind of camaraderie that amateur radio operators have enjoyed for years.

But the Net offered so much more. Storehouses of information. Worldwide "tours" without leaving home. And for marketing, the Net is no less than remarkable because it can be used to establish one-to-one relationships in a global marketplace.

The Internet brings together two of the most powerful trends going on in marketing today: the trend toward individual, personalized relationships and the trend toward globalization. Here's what makes the Net unique for marketers.

1) The Internet is uncontrolled.

Maybe I should have said "unhindered." But by uncontrolled I mean that the Internet is not a technology someone developed specifically for maximum profits. There are plenty of those to be found, each with their own place.

Pharmaceutical companies, for example, develop new lifesaving medications, then take extreme measures to protect their investment and protect their monopoly. I'm not criticizing or blaming them because in our system they need a substantial reward to help offset the considerable risk of R&D.

The same holds true in the computer hardware world. IBM once tried to control the market for technology through their policy of "bundling." Then Apple tried to protect their technology by claiming "look and feel" was patentable.

It's just a good thing for the sake of the Net that no one can claim to protect this system. The Internet's "uncontrollability" is precisely what is making it accessible and affordable to millions around the world.

2) The Internet is global.

Obviously, you say. But think of the advantages of a global phenomenon like the Net. There are no technical restrictions to international use. Language restrictions, yes. Affordability and penetration of technology, yes. But there is still plenty of technical blue sky.

And the rapidly increasing use of the Internet is already creating global opportunities, getting people to rethink their businesses. Look at how many web sites have been advertised on television and in print beginning around 1994. As long as no one is successful in restricting its international access, the Internet will greatly contribute to the globalization of business activities.

3) The Internet is interactive.

This is the feature that finally brings the Internet home for most of us. We can get information through TV or through books, but we can't talk back. We can't influence or jump into the flow of information. With the Internet, we can.

If you're in Sydney, Australia and you have a question about a statement I made in this book, you can contact me instantly over the Internet, and I can reply. Or we can get on-line together. Soon, we'll be able to chat. I'll see you in my screen and you'll see me in yours. (You probably won't want me there for long, however.)

If you convince me I'm wrong on a point in this manuscript, or if you have an interesting point to add, I can change the text and incorporate your comments in the updated version. The next reader, reading this book on the Net or down-loading it, will get the benefit of the update, thanks to you. Once we start to produce books this way the simple linearity of the past will seem far, far away.

4) The Internet is user-controlled.

The previous point about feedback leads to this point; here's the real power and the real secret. The viewer controls. It's not like sitting in church waiting for the sermon to end (talk about linear). If you're tired of what I'm giving you, zap, you're gone. If you want to skip a section, zap. If you want to get to the meat of the message, zap again.

This system works for your benefit, but it also works for mine. When information providers know that they can't just coast through the presentation with a captive audience, they'll sharpen their focus. I'd better get you the information you want, entertain you quickly, or get very inspirational — or your patience will wear thin. The Net will force communicators to become audience-centered in a hurry.

Unfortunately, I've seen resistance to this idea already. Businesses using or considering the Internet are concerned that competitors will use their content. Even knowing that the best they have to offer their customers is product information, they are still reluctant to provide it because of how their competitors could use it against them.

It's a reasonable concern. But imagine how much patience customers will have when they search for Internet information only to find a message like, "Please call or fax our company for more information. We don't know who you are and we don't want to just hand this out to everyone." If they're like me, they quickly look somewhere else, rather than try to storm the gates.

Techniques are being developed to control the flow of information, but if there is such risk in releasing information, then the Internet, or Worldwide Web, will not aid marketing efforts. It's a little like being afraid to send out a brochure because you don't know whose hands it will fall into. Then why print one?

Whether it's presentation tools, data capture, the Internet or something else that hasn't yet been invented, New Media tips the communication scales toward the receiver. It puts the remote in their hands. And that means, more than ever before, marketers will have to become servants to the interests and needs of their customers. Serve or die. Or at least get lost in cyberspace.

10

Focus: Keeping
Sight of What's Important

*Commitment to the "right few" is at the heart of this message, as it is at the heart of
most business success. This chapter demonstrates why it is so hard and
so important to say "no." Strategic planning is not an intellectual
exercise to be accomplished by trained professionals; it's a critical
process for business success and personal satisfaction.*

Chapter summary:

- You can't be all things to all people.
- The Price/Quality Grid.
- Price and quality: A few definitions.
  - Everyone buys value.
  - No one believes you get the highest quality for the lowest price.
  - The middle is usually crowded.
  - The Quadrant of Death.
  - The Discounter.
- What fits for business ...
- The Relationship/Performance Grid.
- Do what you do best and stick with it.
- SWOT yourself.
- The personal element of business: Strategic planning.

After reading this chapter you'll find there are only two really important things
I've had to say, both of which you may have learned a long time ago. But I

encourage you to read on. For as well as you know these two simple ideas, if you have effectively put them into practice you are a rare bird indeed.

Here are the two ideas:

1. You can't be all things to all people.

2. Do what you do best and stick with it.

You may not easily recognize your own difficulty with these ideas, or how they apply to your business. But you may have found yourself on more than one occasion saying about someone else, "If only she could learn to say 'no.' " Or "I can't figure out why he can't stick to the knitting."

We'll look at each of these basic ideas and see how they apply to both our personal and our business decisions.

You can't be all things to all people.

Entrepreneurs are by nature "yes" men and women, but not in the way you might think. They are the polar opposite of employee "yes people," which is exactly why so many entrepreneurs are, well, entrepreneurs. (Often they are terrible employees.)

The difference is that entrepreneurs say "yes" to opportunity. Nothing gets a growth-oriented business owner's blood boiling like a new opportunity. Until they are worn out by the hard reality that things are usually much tougher than they imagined, they ignore the difficulties and look blithely at the optimistic results which they so stubbornly believe in.

Thank God there are people like this and thank God that they often don't let the naysayers stop them in their hope for the future. However, this optimism frequently gets them in trouble. And trouble is normally caused by a simple law of life: When you say "yes" to something you must say "no" to a lot of other things.

You want to have it all. Of course you do. And many have more than most because they refuse to believe that they can't. But another cold, hard law (similar to the laws of economics and gravity) says you simply can't have it all.

Once more, marriage is a perfect illustration. Let's say you wish to marry and there are at least a dozen eligible candidates. Incredibly, they all have the same feelings for you. All have their own attraction. Some have money, some are fun, some physically attractive, and so on. So you ponder.

What about Candidate #1? What opportunity! What a glorious future you can picture! Of course, how can you say anything but "Yes!" Then you consider Candidate #3. Everything you ever wanted. A true soul mate. This can't be missed. You must say "yes." And so on. As long as you say "yes" to a dozen marriage opportunities, you can never truly say yes (unless your idea of bliss is a prison sentence).

Commitment demands saying "no," firmly, resolutely and without regret or looking back. Saying "yes" means saying "no."

Of course, saying "yes" to one career opportunity doesn't mean you will never be able to say "yes" to another. Pursuing one track in your business doesn't mean that another track is out of the question. So it isn't as fixed as the laws against bigamy. However, the mistake usually made is failing to understand that there normally just aren't enough resources available to be fully committed to each "yes." Remove the laws of bigamy and the same principle is at work. If you consider marriage an institution in which each partner ideally meets the needs of the other, polygamy has never worked out very well. Certainly there appear to be men that have found some satisfaction with it. The women, however, invariably feel there aren't enough resources to meet everyone's needs including resources of money, love and marital duties. And unless the husband is totally self-centered, he can hardly be satisfied knowing the pain and misery caused by the unequal distribution of the his resources.

Business opportunities are like that. When resources are limited, each cries for more. So do customers when the company isn't focused. "We need more," they say. "Take care of us better." Or employees complain when management pursues too much. "Give us more," they say.

Some of you may be reading through the lines and hear the quiet voice of personal experience speaking here. My blood boils and my head spins with new entrepreneurial opportunities. And I come by it honestly. My father taught me a lot about saying "yes" and about dealing with change. In my memory as a child and young man growing up, he was a dairy farmer, a TV repairman, an electronics retailer, a travel agent, a manufacturer of background music systems, a radio station owner, a telephone systems dealer, and a real estate developer. So when I started my business I began following a similar path until I found myself with four different businesses, none of which I was managing well, and totally devoid of focus.

In the meantime, my dad, who contracted multiple sclerosis when he was about forty, had used the impending limitations of this disease to focus his life.

Considering he might end up blind or in a wheelchair at any time, and considering he still had young children to care for, he chose real estate development. Using funds from the sale of the main asset he had developed, the radio station, he began building apartments.

My father told me not long ago he spent twenty years of his business life with virtually nothing to show for it. That changed dramatically when he focused. I can assure you, the next twenty years were more than profitable for him.

The need for commitment has personal as well as business applications. People and businesses which lack focus or commitment are relatively easy to spot. Both make a lot of promises they can't keep. They leave disappointed people behind them, from friends to family to customers. And the unfocused business or unfocused person is not fun to watch. They appear to be in pain, always responding to the latest crisis at hand, never appearing to be fully in control of the circumstances of their lives.

Lack of focus in a business may be evident in a variety of ways. An entrepreneurially-dominated business may find itself pursuing promising but totally unrelated opportunities. Employees come to work in the morning never quite certain if they are going to be in the software business, the car repair business or kicking off an Internet franchise opportunity.

Another way a business can lose focus is by trying to be different things to different people: a sales-dominated business. Sales-dominated businesses are usually run by very good sales people who will do just about anything to make the sale — even if it means recasting the entire company according to the wishes of the last customer. It can drive everyone positively nuts.

The effort to try to please everybody is frequently seen in the split personalities of businesses. Ever see the sign, "Highest Quality, Lowest Price?" No one honestly believes that you can get the highest quality for the lowest price, yet countless businesses seem to think this kind of offer is going to get them the business they want. They believe it is possible to be all things to all people.

Instead, successful businesses in highly competitive markets demonstrate that the key is focus. To be the very best possible to the right few. To select the market carefully and then let no one beat you at that particular game. We discussed this in the chapter on Message, but since we are concentrating on the issue of focus here, it is worthwhile to explore this in a little more detail. In trying to explain this idea to businesses, I came across this little chart which can be quite helpful. Helpful first in determining whether or not you are a focused company. Secondly, in determining where you would really like to be, especially relative to your competitors.

The Price/Quality Grid.

As we discuss this little device, first a warning: this is a simplistic picture of some very complex relationships. You'll find things wrong with it and you'll find the analogies breaking down at various points; nevertheless, it can be extremely useful in seeing where you are and where you need to be.

Price and quality: A few definitions.

Price needs no definition; quality just means everything else that is used by the customer as a purchase criteria other than price. It can be convenience, it can be service, it can be durability, it can be status. The "can be's" are just about endless. The point is that when someone buys something they are always trading one thing off for another and therefore always selecting value.

Everyone buys value.

Value is the relationship in your customer's mind between price and quality. Does the man who buys Corn Flakes at the Seven Eleven get value? Of course. There are times he is willing to trade price for convenience. On another occasion he wouldn't make that choice; then price is the driving concern. Does a person who buys a Lexus or Mercedes get value? You bet. The quality factors they have identified (Ride? Resale value? Status? Safety? Performance?) outweigh the considerable price penalty versus a Hyundai or Geo.

No one believes you get the highest quality for the lowest price.

Our experience and instinct combine to make us skeptical of the claims that the highest quality is available at the lowest cost. We know it can't be true, at least not for long.

Certainly there are times when price and quality come together in surprising ways. When Honda started taking over the U.S. car market they could make a legitimate claim for exceptional quality at exceptionally good prices. The results have been dramatic for them and one result is that Hondas are no longer a bargain.

Technology, however, has twisted our understanding of the relationship between price and value. Buy a computer today and tomorrow they'll have one that will be twice as fast and cost half as much. And the next day it will be the same story again. I think some people still haven't bought their first computer, waiting for prices to stabilize.

The exceptions tend to prove the rule. There IS a relationship between price and quality. The marketer who breaks these rules without being able to support it will find himself without a lot of credibility, the most valuable resource of the marketer.

If this is so logical, and I believe it is, the question remains: Why do so many otherwise-intelligent business people try to fool their customers into believing they are the exception? If someone really does offer the highest quality at the lowest price, there will be no need to advertise. They'll be beating your door down in no time.

Still, the ads continue to scream: "Lowest prices on the highest quality." I remember walking into the Nordstrom store in an upper-income Seattle suburb and being flabbergasted to see a small, neatly printed sign on the cashier's counter: "Ask about our low price guarantee." Fortunately they haven't done this in their advertising and I have yet to see a Nordstrom salesperson carefully explaining that Nordstrom's prices are really the lowest. But no doubt some department or even store manager thought he could blunt some of the company's high price image with that little sign. When this store is beating everyone up with incredible service, what is the point?

The middle is usually crowded.

Customers and businesses congregate in the middle of the grid. It's safest buying some combination of reasonable price and reasonable quality, and for many it seems safest selling that way as well. The problem is that gaining a clear identity is difficult. Where is JC Penney these days? What about Sears? Even K Mart, once firmly entrenched as a discounter, got moved to the middle by club stores and Wal-Mart. Unfortunately, the slide toward the middle has not been an easy or a good thing for K Mart profits.

The Quadrant of Death.

This is easy. If your customers understand that you are offering low quality at high prices, you're dead. Your customers will flock to your competitor at their very first opportunity. The only possible reason you could survive here is that you have no competition or your competition is worse than you.

However, if customers think you are selling them low quality at high prices, but you are not, you have to change things. You have to answer the questions, "Why do they think so?" and "What expectation needs to be adjusted and where did they get this expectation?" But don't waste any time. If you find yourself in this situation, you can begin the long, slow, laborious process of changing perceptions. Expect a long tough slog. And hurry.

The Discounter.

Calling this "Discounter" is probably not appropriate since this word has specific meaning and this designation is for anyone who sells on the basis of price. Contractors who seek work on the basis of competitive bids are "discounters" in this sense. They get the work based on offering the lowest price, although they are then usually expected to do the work with the highest quality.

The result of this crazy set of expectations is that there is often a fight and the lawyers are usually the only winners. If you are competing on the basis of price, you need to be the low cost provider; quality-oriented companies that compete on the basis of "low bid" always fight with this dilemma.

However, competing by staking out a position in this quadrant is not bad, not bad at all. If you have the chance to compete on price and you can offer the quality that people who are price-sensitive want, do it. By all means do it. Price-oriented marketers are often market leaders; if they're not, they usually have the opportunity to become market leaders. But there are constant dangers.

One danger is to tire of the fight to maintain a low cost operational position, especially when you notice that competitors in the "Niche" position are doing quite well.

The second danger is to try to broaden your market by addressing quality expectations. It almost goes without saying that if you are the low price leader, your customers will assume your higher price competitors offer better quality. It may be totally untrue but, as you know by now, perception is reality.

So here's the trap. You know you offer as good or better quality than your higher price competition. But because they are higher priced, customers assume they offer higher quality. You react to your research or customer comments about your "low" quality and feel you have to respond. So you improve quality and find you get no credit.

No credit! No matter what you do, even if you scream quality in your advertising, the other guy always gets the credit. And that will never change, simply because your prices are still lower. In the meantime, in your attempts to improve your quality image, you let costs creep up and you can't maintain your price position. And because you are no longer the price leader, your sales falter. Now you're in no man's land.

Take this little self-test. Find your business on the Price/Quality grid. Then, place your competitors. If you find it much easier to place your competitors than yourself you may have your first clue about the difficulty of focusing.

You might find yourself thinking, "Well, yes, we're mostly this but this customer or these customers do business with us for a different reason and we can't ignore them so we have to be a little of this, too." If so, you're struggling with focus. If you know exactly where you are and you've thought this through a long time ago, chances are you've gotten bored and moved on and aren't even reading this.

What fits for business ...

So far we've been discussing the idea of not being all things to all people primarily on a business level. But this is equally true on a personal level. I think it was Margaret Thatcher who said the key to success was finding what you do best and doing it. That's focus. That requires saying no. It requires commitment to the values and goals that are important to you and avoiding the temptation to bend and mold to the latest demands in front of you. Same as for the business.

Let's take a little closer look at the typical entrepreneur in this age of technology startups.

He or she is an excellent engineer. (I'll use "he" from now on to keep it simple.) He worked for Xybrag Manufacturing for several years and often suggested improvements to existing products and even new product lines, only to have his ideas ignored or stolen by somebody higher up. He watched competitors launch products that he thought of long before. So he struck out on his own.

He designed the product on his kitchen table, built the prototype in his garage, begged friends and relatives for start-up money, set up manufacturing in cheap warehouse space. Now it's going and it's a success. He even overcame the entrepreneur's first great hurdle — coming up with a successful second product. Now he has 133 employees, a buzzing assembly line, lots of growth pains and a market just crying for the next great idea.

But he can't find the time to get on the CAD system and work it out. He comes home exhausted from employee reviews, from dealing with the bank, from arguing with the ad agency. Production is slipping and he knows he has to get in there and fix it.

Besides that, the company's market position is being threatened by competitors with innovative improvements and new products. He hired bright new product designers but they just don't have the feel for the market that he does and can't come up with the creative solutions that come naturally to him. He's increasingly frustrated, angry and short tempered. He can't be in all places at once, people all around him seem to be letting him down and he starts thinking this is no fun and maybe he should get out.

If it's hard for a company to realize it can't be all things to all people, it's even harder for individuals to come to that realization. That's because in the early days of the start-up we relied on ourselves to do everything and take care of everything. And it worked. We knew how to do it. That knowledge keeps us at the center of everything in the business, and so does an ego which tells us we have unique qualifications that can't be duplicated.

We will continue in the center until one of two things happen: our businesses continue to grow and prosper and the tide of overwhelming demand on us flows over until we find ourselves picking and choosing what we will do. Or, the business stops growing because it is choked at the top.

When it comes to commitment and focus on a personal level, however, the Price/Quality grid doesn't work very well. At the risk of grossly oversimplifying an even much more complex equation, let me propose another grid. This one we'll call

The Relationship/Performance Grid.

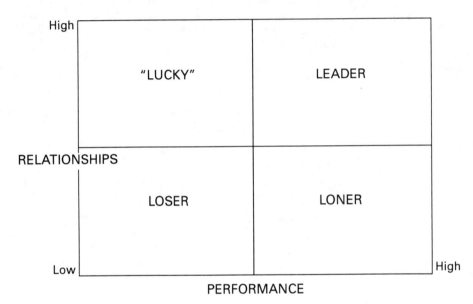

Just as in the Price/Quality grid, there are many places on the Relationship/Performance chart to find success. There is no one right way. The key is to avoid playing all over the board, and the only truly bad spot is the "low/low" corner, when you have no strengths. At the risk of being crude, I've called this grid the "Loser."

If you consider that you have strong relationship skills but consistently disappoint with your performance, consider yourself lucky. Love covers a multitude of sins, even the sins of lack of performance. Your ability to get along with others and to build strong, loyal relationships is a tremendous advantage. You should find work and positions that allow you to play to those strengths and think hard about the performance issues. Truly low performance will ultimately catch up with you and your "luck" will likely fail or at least limit your potential.

The stereotypical loner is the engineer, artist or software programmer who is said to be kept in the back room working forty hours at a stretch with an occasional Big Mac thrown in through the door to keep him going. We're living in an age of the phenomenally successful "geeks," but let's not be fooled. While there are definitely rewards for high performance without relationship skills, there is no doubt that the world belongs to those who can lead. And that requires both high performance and high relationship abilities.

Back in the Price/Quality grid, if you found yourself on dangerous ground (high price image without a corresponding high quality image) then you could chart a new direction. But there are a number of good positions to be at with this chart, mostly running on a diagonal line from low/low to high/high.

The same cannot be said for the Relationship/Performance chart. Low/low is simply not a good position, because it usually means low/low pay and lower/lower expectations. So use this chart to help you understand where you are. Then chart out your next move, keeping in mind that you cannot be all things to all people. Concentrate on helping the right few (maybe like a spouse, your children and your supervisor) place an exceptionally high value on what you do.

By now we understand that success is not based on being the very best at everything. Jack-of-all trades, master of none isn't good enough, anymore. It doesn't work very well for businesses in crowded markets and it doesn't work very well for individuals trying to find their place in a workplace with jobs in short supply. We've also established that you can't choose without going through the painful process of saying "no." Without "no," in reality there is no "yes."

But, how do you get to the "yes?" How do you make the right choice amidst all the wonderful opportunities in front of you? Making those choices is what strategic planning is all about. For businesses and personal life, it comes down to a process of matching up two things: Your strengths with the needs of the right few.

Do what you do best and stick with it.

Business owners or managers often become so enamored with the opportunities all around them that they have a difficult time deciding where to focus. That's when they call in the strategic planning experts. Frequently it is a good idea because the outside perspective can be very helpful. But the process of providing this help is really remarkably simple.

Here's what I do in this situation.

Me: So, as I understand it, you want to focus your resources where they will do you the most good, right?

Executive Team: Right.

Me: First, let's make a list on this white board of your key customers or key customer categories. And let's put an "A" by each customer or customer group that is the very most important to you.

Executive Team: (List)

Me: Now let's list the services or products you offer. And let's put an "A" by the products or services that make you the most money.

Executive Team: (List)

Me: What products or services do the top customers place the highest value on? The "A"s? Good, then that's what we can focus on right now. But before we decide on this, let's look at the future. Let's make another list of all the things that are possible for this company to do, either with existing resources or with resources that could reasonably be added to the company.

Executive Team: Shouldn't we start with listing who our potential key customers could and should be?

Me: My goodness, you're right. We should always start with the customers.

Executive Team: (Lists potential key customers or existing customers with more potential. Then lists all potential products and services).

Me: Now, if we were to offer these services, what would our key customers place the highest value on? Place an "A" by those.

Executive Team: But it will mean we have to change to offer those and it will cost a lot of time and money.

Me: Cost more than the long-term benefit?

Executive Team: Well, no.

Me: Then it's your choice, right?

Executive Team: But if we focus on those things, it will take up resources that could be used for all these other things.

Me: Will doing all these other things reward you more than focusing on where you can get the highest return and where your key customers place the highest value?

Executive Team: Well, no, but ...

Me: But, what?

Executive Team: Well, I guess we like the idea of being all things to all people, even if it doesn't make sense.

Me: Then your plan is to choose to not be strategic, right?

Them: Right.

Of course, it never goes like that. But seriously, it is often a difficult struggle to choose those directions that will logically and clearly point to the greatest return. It's called decision making and precious few are really good at it. When the media, unions and workers complain about high executive compensation, it is usually because they do not know the real skill, talent, knowledge and instinct that go into real-life decision making.

In the book, *The Discipline of Market Leaders*, Fred Wiersema and Michael Treacy effectively point out that there is more than one path to business success and market leadership. But whether it is a conscious process or not, priorities are selected and consistently maintained. The priority may be a price discipline, or innovation, or operational excellence, or customer intimacy. But whatever is chosen eliminates the other choices as priorities and the company's success hinges on the consistent application of its chosen priority.

SWOT yourself.

The common technique used by many strategic planning professionals and businesses is the SWOT analysis. Like the previous example, the magic is in listing all the options on paper, getting some good, knowledgeable minds together and simply analyzing each of the options around two questions:

1. Where is the value?

2. What do we do best?

If you haven't gone through this exercise before, have a little fun. Call your management team together at some nice oceanside resort. Get a big pad of paper and some felt pens and make four headings: Strengths, Weaknesses, Opportunities, Threats.

You'll find you will spend half your time arguing about which column various items fit in, but that's a different problem. It's actually very enlightening. If you go through this with a group from your business, here's what you will likely find.

You will come up with a long list of strengths but only about two or three will really be consistent and important. Most everyone will agree with those two or three. Then you'll look at the opportunities and you will likely find that there are a number of very good opportunities that line up with your existing strengths. There will be some good opportunities that line up better with your weaknesses and a number that don't have much to do with you at all. Scratch off all strengths and opportunities other than those two or three that really count.

You may have a long list of weaknesses, but probably very few that really counteract your strengths. Unless they are critical to your existence, forget them. Threats can be divided into those things you can control and those you can't. Threats you can control are likely also to be found in your weaknesses. You've already dealt with those.

So what do you have left? Strengths and corresponding opportunities. Simple. Now you know what to do. Strategic planning is done. Implementation is left and unfortunately, that's the really tough part.

The personal element of business: Strategic planning.

One of the things you will likely discover as you go through this strategic planning process is, you can't separate the people involved from the process. At first, the process may appear to be just a matter of logic and analysis. In reality, personality and personal preferences weigh heavily in the process.

You will find a strong relationship between the strengths the company is focusing on and the strengths of the individuals doing the focusing. And you will find a strong parallel between the future opportunities that become your focal point and the ideas and convictions that individuals have about the nature of the future. But that shouldn't be too surprising. After all, companies aren't buildings and computers and machines. They are collections of individuals.

This fact is critically important when it comes to implementing your strategic plan. There's a lot of talk about "ownership." Key employees need to "own" the plan if they are to make it work. That's absolutely true. Effort given in a direction in which there is no conviction simply doesn't accomplish anywhere near the same amount of work. Another way of putting it is that personal priorities must align with company priorities. It's the whole "alignment of goals" thing again.

With this in mind, I usually start the strategic planning process with some personal strategic planning. That means asking each individual involved: Where's your focus? What's really important to you? What do you really want from life?

It should be so easy. It seems people ought to be able to say: Here's where my heart is really centered, here's what is important in my life, here's where my strengths and gifts and personal interests are, here's what I want my life to mean when it is all over. But, of course, it is exceedingly difficult. It's that old saying "yes" and "no" thing again. Too many things to say "yes" to, too many reasons to not want to say "no."

There are two parts to setting a personal focus: What we believe ought to be and what really is. Sort of like perception and reality, or being and becoming. Business is an excellent analogy.

In the strategic planning process, the business planning team decides that it needs to focus on a certain direction. It's logical, clear, smart, the right thing to do. Then they get back together in a year and find out they really haven't done anything to make it different. Things are pretty much the same. The planning has meant nothing, and the reason for this is simple: there are other forces at work. The strategic plan is somehow conflicting with the reality of how decisions are actually being made.

A business wants to expand and knows that it must disperse management authority and responsibility. It makes the decision to do that, then two years later realizes it hasn't happened. Why? Because those who held responsibility and authority couldn't let it go. That's reality. It's what they really want — not what makes sense, not what they know in their heart is right for them and the company — but it is the only thing they are comfortable with, so they hang on.

Another example: It becomes clear that a company needs to abandon an old handcrafted way of producing its product and move to more efficient production techniques. It buys the equipment, trains people, projects the improvements in its business plan.

But two years later, most of the production is still done the old way. Why? Because the person in charge is only comfortable with that. It's what he knows, he learned it from his dad and can't imagine his long dead father approving of anything less than hands on. It runs deep, to the very heart. It can't be changed without great pain and personal cost. This is reality.

So if you are serious about doing personal strategic planning and coming up with a personal focus, be honest and look at reality. If you find something deep and ingrained, do not think it cannot be changed. At the same time, don't fool yourself into thinking that logic and careful analysis and decision making are enough.

If a desire to please others is close to your heart, recognize it and use it. If acceptance based on your hard work and productivity has been the driving force, don't look to change it so much as harness it productively. If you base your need for respect on other's perception of your smarts and wisdom, then incorporate that deep-seated need into your personal strengths and weaknesses evaluation.

There is a common theme here, based on my conviction that at the deepest level we are all motivated by one thing: the need for love, acceptance and respect. We just have a zillion different ways of pursuing those things. And we have even more ways of protecting ourselves against the pain of failure in that search. Understanding and accepting our personal style of gaining love and acceptance is a key to the reality I've been referring to.

As long as we pay attention to reality, it's time to try a personal strategic plan. We said when talking about business strategic plans it was a matter of matching up two things: The right few with your greatest strengths.

We said that successful marketing is helping the right few place a high value on what you do. Now the same can be said of successful personal living. Especially if we are really focusing on the right few.

Start a column on your white board. Title it, "The Right Few." List as many as you can think of. Put an "A" by the ones that are really important. If you have a hard time coming up with the list, here are a few categories you might consider:

God

Family

Friends

Supervisors

Co-workers

Customers

The next column should be titled "Value." What value do I bring to those right few? What do they value from me and what do I have to offer? Put an "A" by the products or services you offer that deliver the highest value. If you have a hard time coming up with the right priorities, now is a good time to really try the little exercise I mentioned once before: Go to the cemetery where you will likely be buried.

Look at the headstones of those whose bones now rest there. Reflect for awhile. They too were preoccupied in their lives with priorities they believed to be vitally important — things you can only now imagine. They too felt stress and anxiety. Just like you, they seldom considered the shortness of their lives, seldom paused to wonder what someone would write on their grave markers.

Now that your head has been cleared by that little exercise, go back and reconsider your list of "the right few" and the list of the values you offer. You may discover that the time spent with your son or daughter or wife or husband tends to take a little higher priority. And it's not that you need to do more for them. God knows you're working hard and doing all you can. It's probably that they need a little more of your time, your focused attention, your interest in what's important to them, your life, yourself.

You may also discover that people you work with are also valuable to you. Your precious days are spent with them. You share hopes, dreams, goals, laughs, victories and defeats. But you may discover that the real value you bring to them is not your marketing skills, your leadership abilities, or your organizing talents. It may be more how you make them feel about themselves, whether or not you make their day go a little easier, how you are helping them learn and develop into being all that they can be as contributing, positive people.

To do that, you may find you have to change a little. Let go of some things that you think are terribly important but now you realize in the overall scheme of things, don't really matter that much. Maybe you begin to understand that the stresses and strains you feel do not need to be imposed on others.

As you reflect on who the important people are in your life, and what value you can bring to them, the many issues we've dealt with in this book can be reduced to a single point of crystal-clear focus. It is a singular truth, so remarkably simple that we know in our hearts it must be right.

We've discovered that business success comes down to relationships, and relationships come down to a willingness to sacrifice our own needs in order to satisfy our customer's needs. And now we've discovered on a personal level that the value we can offer others ultimately comes down to our willingness to give up some of our own desires for personal fulfillment. That's the only way to take care of the deep needs of those we most care about.

But we don't want to. And it runs counter to almost everything we hear today. "Take care of yourself," the psychologists say. They seldom, if ever, tell you that the real path to taking care of yourself is through service. "Look out for the bottom line," young business people are taught to believe. But the smart ones, the successful ones, understand that looking out for their friends IS looking out for their bottom line.

Not long ago, my small group of friends went through the exercise of trying to write personal mission statements. It caused me to consider what was important and how I should prioritize my life. The only mission statement I could come up with was this: "To hear the words, `Well done, good and faithful servant.' " I deeply believe my success, business and personal, will be measured by how seriously I take that mission.

*"It is not enough to be busy; so are the ants. The
question is: What are we busy about?"*
— Henry David Thoreau

11

Don't Look for Balance
at the End of this Book

I used to think the trick to handling life was to find balance. Balance all those competing interests that pull at you and find the middle point among them. Find a compromise, somewhere in between. Equilibrium was the word I used as the focal point of this effort.

So when a group of friends came together, men in similar circumstances in life and with similar values and interests, I suggested we informally name our group "Equilibrium." All of us seemed to be searching for the same balance point.

To us, equilibrium meant finding middle ground among competing interests such as the desire for a strong, loving family and the desire for a successful, growing business. Between our desire for a relationship with God that we all believed should be at the center of our lives and the impulse we felt to put heart and soul into our work.

For over five years we wrestled with these issues, even while dealing with life crises such as marital infidelity, cancer, clinical depression, business reversals, and the dilemmas of a highly successful business sale. All the while, however, equilibrium eluded us.

There was a reason, but it took time to discover. And if you've read this book, I think you may understand what we learned a little more quickly.

Equilibrium, it turns out, wasn't really possible in the first place. There's no equilibrium on a see-saw as children tip back and forth. There's no equilibrium between two aggressive armies. And there's no equilibrium on the job.

The answer we were looking for wasn't equilibrium, it was *integration*. It was to find your core values and align everything with them. To take the disjointed parts of our lives and bring them all together on the same channel. That's what I wanted to explain on every page of this book.

In the end, does the desire to develop meaningful friendships interfere with the desire to build a successful business? Not when you understand that the goals and methods are the same. Not when you realize that the best and most enjoyable way to build your business is to concentrate on strengthening and building new relationships. And not when you understand that family and business needn't conflict when relationships are at the heart of business.

True, you can't have it all. Equilibrium is a sort of sad acknowledgment of that, and a settling for an uninspired compromise.

Integration, on the other hand, is a way of embracing the best, the most important with the understanding that not everything is of equal importance in your life. Something must give, and your core values determine what those things are. But there is no real sadness in giving up less significant pursuits when you know that you are choosing something better.

So go ahead and choose! Bring the best parts of your life back to work. Have fun. Make friends on the job. I guarantee it will change the way you do business. And it will certainly change the way you live.

Index

A

alignment of goals, viii-x, 47, 92, 115, 178
assets, 5
audience, 81-84, 140, 143-144, 150, 156
awareness, 43, 47, 52, 134-135, 147

B

Bernbach, Bill, 65
Blanchard, Kenneth, 103
business relationships,
    four elements of, 43, 47-57

C

chemistry, 43, 47, 56, 130, 134-135
communication
    purposes of, 146-147
communication tools, 161
    seven checkpoints for building, 137, 147-152
compensation, 91, 101, 104-108, 111-113, 115
competition, 6, 29-30, 63-64, 69-71, 86, 119, 171-172
core message of a business, 59-61, 65-67, 86, 144

reasons for, 59, 61-65
steps to building, 59, 67-76
credibility, 43, 47, 49, 50-52, 55, 134-135, 144, 170
customers, 3-11, 16, 18, 20-22, 32, 38-40, 48, 51, 55, 60, 65, 67-73, 76-77, 80, 85-86, 97-98, 109-111, 115, 117, 126-127, 138, 141, 144, 160
    key, viii, 8, 43, 47, 159, 176
customer check-ups, 40-41

D

Drucker, Pete, 4

E

80/20 rule, 7, 19, 27-29, 126
editorial environment, 83-84
equity of a business, 1, 4, 49

F

feedback, 34-35, 95, 163
focus groups, 39-40, 42
Ford, Henry, 158
friendship, ix, xi, xiii, 12, 15-16, 22, 26, 32, 43- 45, 57, 124, 135, 161-164
    costs of, 45-46
    definition of, 46-47

Friendship Marketing, viii, 1, 62, 91, 97-99, 114-115, 137, 139
  seven principles of, 4-14

H

hearing, 27, 38-41

G

grassroots polling, 38, 42

I

influencers, viii, 115, 116
Internet, 138, 139, 157, 161-164

K

key relationships, 6, 7, 49, 81, 117

L

Lewis, C.S., 43, 44, 46
listening, viii-x, 15-29, 32, 34, 37-38, 41-42, 71, 79, 92, 115, 123, 129, 131, 140

M

marketing tools, 137-164
  objectives of, 144
McKenna, Regis, 97, 158
measurement, 91, 101-102
media, the, 20, 67, 77-79, 177
  rules for dealing with, 77, 79-89

N

Net, the, see Internet
New Media, the, 137-138, 152-164
note-taking, 33-34

O

Ogilvy, David, 10

P

Peters, Tom, 40
Postman, Neil, 155
"Power and the Glory, The," x, 91, 97-98

presentation tools, 160-161, 164
price, 3, 11, 49, 52, 62-64, 68-71, 86, 87, 131-132, 134, 165, 168-172, 177
Price/Quality Grid, The, 70, 165, 169, 172, 174-175
profit, 4-5, 15, 30, 107, 127
prospects, 31, 37, 39-40, 49, 117, 126-127, 134-135, 138, 140, 143-144, 157, 160

Q

Quadrant of Death, the, 165, 171
quality, 5, 11, 64, 68-71, 86, 165, 168-172
questions, 36-37

R

recognition, 91, 101, 103, 106
Relationship/Performance Grid, 165, 174-175
Ries, Al, 66
"right few, the," viii, 69, 87, 98, 144, 165, 168, 175, 180-181

S

saints, 117, 128
SALT Principles, vii, x, 92, 114
savables, 117, 128
selling, 117, 118, 142, 147
  basics of, 117-135
Senge, Peter, 98, 112
sinners, 117, 128
strategic planning, 165, 175, 178-180
strategic relationships, viii, x, 1, 10, 85, 92, 97, 108, 115
surveys, formal, 41-42
suspects, 117, 126, 127
SWOT analysis, 165, 177-178

T

teamwork, viii, x, 91-92, 97-98, 103, 116
Treacy, Michael, 177

Trout, Jack, 66

trust, 43, 47, 52-53, 55-56, 61-62, 67, 134-135

U

Unique Selling Proposition (USP), 66

V

value
of a business, viii, xii, 5-6, 8, 11-12, 48-49, 68, 111, 177, 180-182
related to price and quality of a product, 5, 169-170

W

Walton, Sam, 40
Wiersema, Fred, 177
WIIFM, 2, 22
winning, 91, 99-101, 112-113, 115-116
word ownership, 66
Wurman, Richard Saul, 152

Additional Friendship Marketing Resources

Friendship Marketing's SALT Principles: Seasoning the Business of Life
by Gerald Baron © *1997*   *Published by Quest Enterprise Institute*
paperback, $9.95/$60 for a package of 10 copies
Inquiries/Orders: **(360) 671-8708** (9am - 5pm PST)
This pocket-sized volume summarizes all the key elements of Friendship Marketing in a concise, quick-read format. Ideal for handouts or company study groups.

The SALT Principles Presentation Kit
Published by Quest Enterprise Institute
complete kit, $295
Inquiries/Orders: : **(360) 671-8708** (9am - 5pm PST)
A complete workbook kit enabling you to present the SALT Principles in your business. Includes a PowerPoint™ presentation, color overheads, worksheets, presentation notes, exercises.

Friendship Marketing Seminars and Workshops

Conducted by Gerald Baron and Bill Palmer
Call Quest Enterprise Institute (360) 671-8708 for pricing.

On-Site SALT Audit.
Gerald or Bill will spend a full day at your business, meeting with key personnel and gauging how Friendship Marketing can help your staff change the way they do business. At the end of the audit, you will receive a full report with their findings, including ways to implement Friendship Marketing on a larger scale.

Semiahmoo Forum.
Gerald and Bill will train business leaders and executives in the principles of Friendship Marketing at the Pacific Northwest's premiere waterfront/golf resort. The Thursday through Sunday forum allows time for small group discussion and sharing of ideas, as well as developing Friendship Marketing implementation plans. Golf, tennis, swimming, charter fishing, whale-watching, salmon bakes and much more make Semiahmoo the ideal work/play destination.

Friendship Marketing In-House Workshop.
This five-day, in-house program is the ultimate forum for training your entire staff and implementing Friendship Marketing principles on every level. Gerald or Bill will guide staff members through a customized series of individual seminars, small group sessions, individual coaching and follow-up. Custom workshops of varying length may also be arranged. Call for details.

Friendship Marketing Online.   *http://www.baron-co.com/fm*

Visit Friendship Marketing's web site for the latest articles, seminar information, updates and related material.

THE OASIS PRESS® ORDER FORM

Call, Mail, or Fax Your Order to: PSI Research, 300 North Valley Drive, Grants Pass, OR 97526 USA
Order Phone USA & Canada: +1 800 228-2275   **Inquiries & International Orders:** +1 541 479-9464   **Fax:** +1 541 476-1479

TITLE	✔ BINDER	✔ PAPERBACK	QUANTITY	COST
Bottom Line Basics	☐ $39.95	☐ $19.95		
The Business Environmental Handbook	☐ $39.95	☐ $19.95		
Business Owner's Guide to Accounting & Bookkeeping		☐ $19.95		
Buyer's Guide to Business Insurance	☐ $39.95	☐ $19.95		
Collection Techniques for a Small Business	☐ $39.95	☐ $19.95		
A Company Policy and Personnel Workbook	☐ $49.95	☐ $29.95		
Company Relocation Handbook	☐ $39.95	☐ $19.95		
CompControl: The Secrets of Reducing Worker's Compensation Costs	☐ $39.95	☐ $19.95		
Complete Book of Business Forms	☐ $39.95	☐ $19.95		
Customer Engineering: Cutting Edge Selling Strategies	☐ $39.95	☐ $19.95		
Develop & Market Your Creative Ideas		☐ $15.95		
Doing Business in Russia		☐ $19.95		
Draw The Line: A Sexual Harassment Free Workplace		☐ $17.95		
The Essential Corporation Handbook		☐ $19.95		
The Essential Limited Liability Company Handbook	☐ $39.95	☐ $19.95		
Export Now: A Guide for Small Business	☐ $39.95	☐ $19.95		
Financial Management Techniques for Small Business	☐ $39.95	☐ $19.95		
Financing Your Small Business		☐ $19.95		
Franchise Bible: How to Buy a Franchise or Franchise Your Own Business	☐ $39.95	☐ $19.95		
Friendship Marketing *Availble in Spring 1997!*		☐ $18.95		
Home Business Made Easy		☐ $19.95		
Incorporating Without A Lawyer *(Available for 32 states)* SPECIFY STATE:		☐ $24.95		
Joysticks, Blinking Lights and Thrills *Availble in Spring 1997!*		☐ $18.95		
The Insider's Guide to Small Business Loans	☐ $29.95	☐ $19.95		
InstaCorp – Incorporate In Any State (Book & Software) *New for 1997!*		☐ $29.95		
Keeping Score: An Insider Look at Sports Marketing		☐ $18.95		
Know Your Market: How to Do Low-Cost Market Research	☐ $39.95	☐ $19.95		
Legal Expense Defense: How to Control Your Business' Legal Costs and Problems	☐ $39.95	☐ $19.95		
Location, Location, Location: How To Select The Best Site For Your Business		☐ $19.95		
Mail Order Legal Guide	☐ $45.00	☐ $29.95		
Managing People: A Practical Guide		☐ $19.95		
Marketing Mastery: Your Seven Step Guide to Success	☐ $39.95	☐ $19.95		
The Money Connection: Where and How to Apply for Business Loans and Venture Capital	☐ $39.95	☐ $19.95		
People Investment	☐ $39.95	☐ $19.95		
Power Marketing for Small Business	☐ $39.95	☐ $19.95		
Profit Power: 101 Pointers ro Give Your Small Business A Competitive Edge	☐ $39.95	☐ $19.95		
Proposal Development: How to Respond and Win the Bid	☐ $39.95	☐ $19.95		
Raising Capital	☐ $39.95	☐ $19.95		
Retail in Detail: How to Start and Manage a Small Retail Business		☐ $14.95		
Secrets to Buying and Selling a Business *New for 1997!*		☐ $19.95		
Secure Your Future: Financial Planning at Any Age	☐ $39.95	☐ $19.95		
The Small Business Insider's Guide to Bankers *Availble in Spring 1997!*		☐ $18.95		
Start Your Business *(Available as a book and disk package – see back)*		☐ $ 9.95 (without disk)		
Starting and Operating a Business in... book INCLUDES FEDERAL section PLUS ONE STATE section		☐ $29.95	☐	$24.95
PLEASE SPECIFY WHICH STATE(S) YOU WANT:				
STATE SECTION ONLY (BINDER NOT INCLUDED) SPECIFY STATE(S):	☐ $8.95			
FEDERAL SECTION ONLY (BINDER NOT INCLUDED)	☐ $12.95			
U.S. EDITION (FEDERAL SECTION – 50 STATES AND WASHINGTON DC IN 11-BINDER SET)	☐ $295.95			
Successful Business Plan: Secrets & Strategies	☐ $49.95	☐ $24.95		
Successful Network Marketing for The 21st Century		☐ $14.95		
Surviving and Prospering in a Business Partnership	☐ $39.95	☐ $19.95		
TargetSmart! Database Marketing for the Small Business		☐ $19.95		
Top Tax Saving Ideas for Today's Small Business		☐ $15.95		
Which Business? Help in Selecting Your New Venture		☐ $18.95		
Write Your Own Business Contracts	☐ $39.95	☐ $19.95		

BOOK SUB-TOTAL (FIGURE YOUR TOTAL AMOUNT ON THE OTHER SIDE)

OASIS SOFTWARE   Please check Macintosh or 3-1/2" Disk for IBM-PC & Compatibles

TITLE	3-1/2" IBM Disk	Mac-OS	Price	QUANTITY	COST
California Corporation Formation Package ASCII Software	☐	☐	$ 39.95		
Company Policy & Personnel Software Text Files	☐	☐	$ 49.95		
Financial Management Techniques (Full Standalone)	☐		$ 99.95		
Financial Templates	☐	☐	$ 69.95		
The Insurance Assistant Software (Full Standalone)	☐		$ 29.95		
Start A Business (Full Standalone)	☐		$ 49.95		
Start Your Business (Software for Windows™)	☐		$ 19.95		
Successful Business Plan (Software for Windows™)	☐		$ 99.95		
Successful Business Plan Templates	☐	☐	$ 69.95		
The Survey Genie - Customer Edition (Full Standalone)	☐		$149.95		
The Survey Genie - Employee Edition (Full Standalone)	☐		$149.95		
SOFTWARE SUB-TOTAL					

BOOK & DISK PACKAGES   Please check whether you use Macintosh or 3-1/2" Disk for IBM-PC & Compatibles

TITLE	IBM-PC	Mac-OS	BINDER	PAPERBACK	QUANTITY	COST
The Buyer's Guide to Business Insurance w/ Insurance Assistant	☐		☐ $ 59.95	☐ $ 39.95		
California Corporation Formation Binder Book & ASCII Software	☐	☐	☐ $ 69.95	☐ $ 59.95		
Company Policy & Personnel Book & Software Text Files	☐	☐	☐ $ 89.95	☐ $ 69.95		
Financial Management Techniques Book & Software	☐		☐ $ 129.95	☐ $ 119.95		
Start Your Business Paperback & Software (Software for Windows™)	☐			☐ $ 24.95		
Successful Business Plan Book & Software for Windows™	☐		☐ $125.95	☐ $109.95		
Successful Business Plan Book & Software Templates	☐	☐	☐ $109.95	☐ $ 89.95		
BOOK & DISK PACKAGE TOTAL						

AUDIO CASSETTES

TITLE	Price	QUANTITY	COST
Power Marketing Tools For Small Business	☐ $ 49.95		
The Secrets To Buying & Selling A Business	☐ $ 49.95		
AUDIO CASSETTE SUB-TOTAL			

OASIS SUCCESS KITS   Call for more information about these products

TITLE	Price	QUANTITY	COST
Start-Up Success Kit	☐ $ 39.95		
Business At Home Success Kit	☐ $ 39.95		
Financial Management Success Kit	☐ $ 44.95		
Personnel Success Kit	☐ $ 44.95		
Marketing Success Kit	☐ $ 44.95		
OASIS SUCCESS KITS TOTAL			

COMBINED SUB-TOTAL (FROM THIS SIDE)

SOLD TO: *Please give street address*

NAME:

Title:

Company:

Street Address:

City/State/Zip:

Daytime Phone: Email:

SHIP TO: *If different than above give street address*

NAME:

Title:

Company:

Street Address:

City/State/Zip:

Daytime Phone:

PAYMENT INFORMATION: *Rush service is available, call for details.*
International and Canadian Orders: Please call for quote on shipping.

☐ CHECK Enclosed payable to PSI Research

Card Number:

Signature:

YOUR GRAND TOTAL

SUB-TOTALS (from other side) $

SUB-TOTALS (from this side) $

SHIPPING (see chart below) $

TOTAL ORDER $

If your purchase is:	Shipping costs within the USA:
$0 - $25	$5.00
$25.01 - $50	$6.00
$50.01 - $100	$7.00
$100.01 - $175	$9.00
$175.01 - $250	$13.00
$250.01 - $500	$18.00
$500.01+	4% of total merchandise

Charge: ☐ VISA   ☐ MASTERCARD   ☐ AMEX   ☐ DISCOVER

Expires:

Name On Card:

KYMK0197

Call toll free to order 1-800-228-2275 PSI Research 300 North Valley Drive, Grants Pass, OR 97526 FAX 541-476-1479

Friendship Marketing: Growing your business by cultivating strategic relationships

This book format is:
- ☐ Binder book
- ☐ Paperback book
- ☐ Book/Software Combination
- ☐ Software only

Rate this product's overall quality of information:
- ☐ Excellent
- ☐ Good
- ☐ Fair
- ☐ Poor

Rate the quality of printed materials:
- ☐ Excellent
- ☐ Good
- ☐ Fair
- ☐ Poor

Rate the format:
- ☐ Excellent
- ☐ Good
- ☐ Fair
- ☐ Poor

Did the product provide what you needed?
- ☐ Yes ☐ No

If not, what should be added?
_____
_____
_____
_____

This product is:
- ☐ Clear and easy to follow
- ☐ Too complicated
- ☐ Too elementary

Were the worksheets (if any) easy to use?
- ☐ Yes ☐ No ☐ N/A

Should we include?
- ☐ More worksheets
- ☐ Fewer worksheets
- ☐ No worksheets

How do you feel about the price?
- ☐ Lower than expected
- ☐ About right
- ☐ Too expensive

How many employees are in your company?
- ☐ Under 10 employees
- ☐ 10 - 50 employees
- ☐ 51 - 99 employees
- ☐ 100 - 250 employees
- ☐ Over 250 employees

How many people in the city your company is in?
- ☐ 50,000 - 100,000
- ☐ 100,000 - 500,000
- ☐ 500,000 - 1,000,000
- ☐ Over 1,000,000
- ☐ Rural (Under 50,000)

What is your type of business?
- ☐ Retail
- ☐ Service
- ☐ Government
- ☐ Manufacturing
- ☐ Distributor
- ☐ Education

What types of products or services do you sell?
_____
_____

What is your position in the company?
(please check one)
- ☐ Owner
- ☐ Administrative
- ☐ Sales/Marketing
- ☐ Finance
- ☐ Human Resources
- ☐ Production
- ☐ Operations
- ☐ Computer/MIS

How did you learn about this product?
- ☐ Recommended by a friend
- ☐ Used in a seminar or class
- ☐ Have used other PSI products
- ☐ Received a mailing
- ☐ Saw in bookstore
- ☐ Saw in library
- ☐ Saw review in:
  - ☐ Newspaper
  - ☐ Magazine
  - ☐ Radio/TV

Where did you buy this product?
- ☐ Catalog
- ☐ Bookstore
- ☐ Office supply
- ☐ Consultant

Would you purchase other business tools from us?
- ☐ Yes ☐ No

If so, which products interest you?
- ☐ EXECARDS® Communications Tools
- ☐ Books for business
- ☐ Software

Would you recommend this product to a friend?
- ☐ Yes ☐ No

Do you use a personal computer?
- ☐ Yes ☐ No

If yes, which?
- ☐ Macintosh
- ☐ IBM/compatible

Check all the ways you use computers?
- ☐ Word processing
- ☐ Accounting
- ☐ Spreadsheet
- ☐ Inventory
- ☐ Order processing
- ☐ Design/Graphics
- ☐ General Data Base
- ☐ Customer Information
- ☐ Scheduling

May we call you to follow up on your comments?
- ☐ Yes ☐ No

May we add your name to our mailing list? ☐ Yes ☐ No

If you'd like us to send associates or friends a catalog, just list names and addresses on back.

Is there anything we should do to improve our products?
_____

Just fill in your name and address here, fold (see back) and mail.

Name _____

Title _____

Company _____

Phone _____

Address _____

City/State/Zip _____

E Mail Address (Home) _____ (Business) _____

FM97

If you have friends or associates who might appreciate receiving our catalogs, please list here. Thanks!

Name_____   Name_____

Title_____   Title_____

Company_____   Company_____

Phone_____   Phone_____

Address_____   Address_____

Address_____   Address_____

FOLD HERE FIRST

NO POSTAGE
NECESSARY
IF MAILED
IN THE
UNITED STATES

BUSINESS REPLY MAIL

FIRST CLASS MAIL PERMIT NO. 002 MERLIN, OREGON

POSTAGE WILL BE PAID BY ADDRESSEE

PSI Research
PO BOX 1414
Merlin OR 97532-9900

FOLD HERE SECOND, THEN TAPE TOGETHER

✂
Please cut
along this
vertical line,
fold twice,
tape together
and mail.